CONTENTS

Front cover: Harlech Castle

Fresh, green hills and whitewashed farmstead – a typical M

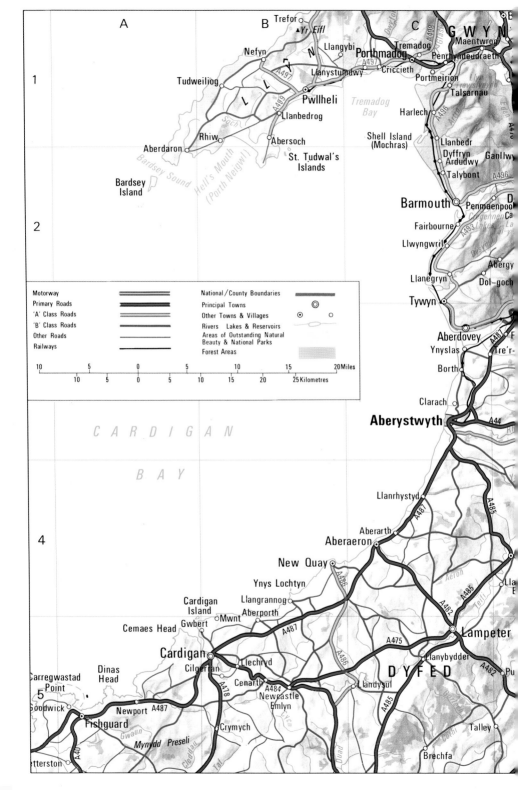

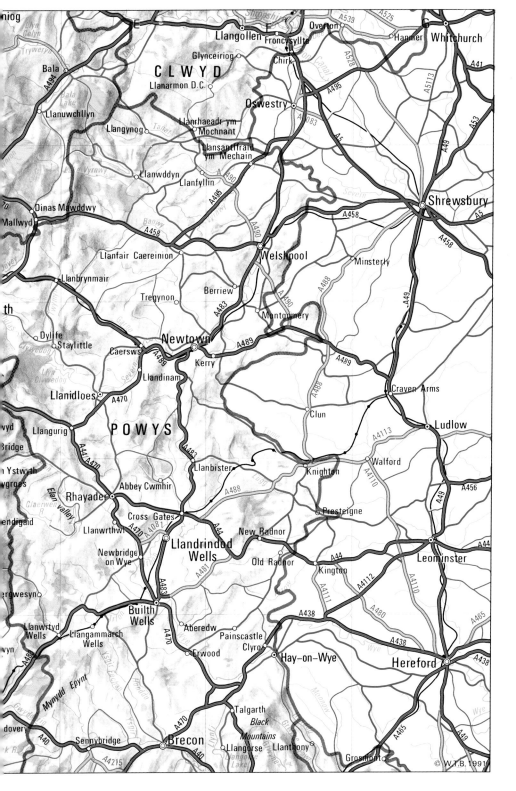

WHERE TO GO – AT A GLANCE

For quick, easy reference, here is a list of all the attractions and places to visit featured in this book together with the pages on which you'll find the relevant information.

Felin Geri Flour Mill

Portmeirion

Meirion Woollen Mill

National Centre for Alternative Technology

Talyllyn Railway

Powis Castle gardens

The A–Z gazetteer of resorts, cities, towns and villages starts here. It's all laid out in an informative, easy-to-follow style. Each entry contains a description of the destination in question followed by a list of its attractions and places to visit. These range from narrow-gauge railways to woollen mills, wildlife centres to leisure parks, castles to forest visitor centres. Mid Wales also has its unusual places to visit – call in at a 'village of the future' dedicated to alternative technology and self-sufficiency, or a silver-lead mine open to the public.

Attractions and places to visit are highlighted in **bold italic** at the end of each entry. It is impossible, in a guide of this nature, to give precise opening details for each attraction. The vast majority will be open at all reasonable hours from April to the end of September.

Many will also stay open (often on a limited basis) in the winter months. Telephone numbers are provided, so you can check for yourself – or call into a Tourist Information Centre for details of local places to visit.

KEY TO SYMBOLS

i   Tourist Information Centre

E4   Each entry has a map reference to enable you to locate it on the gridded Mid Wales map on pages 2/3

C/F (following telephone number): Admission is charged/free. Please note that for some entries – such as castles which can

be viewed from exterior only and cathedrals – it is not appropriate to include C/F information

⊕   Cadw: Welsh Historic Monuments site

🐾   National Trust site

🏛   National Museum of Wales site

ABBEY CWMHIR
POWYS   E4

The forgotten little community of Abbey Cwmhir, away from it all in the folds of forested hills north of Llandrindod Wells, was better known in medieval times. The clues to its past fame lie in the ruins which stand in a field beside the Clywedog brook. These are the remnants of a grand Cistercian abbey, founded in 1143. The fragmentary ruins seem all the more poignant when we discover that Abbey Cwmhir once had by far the largest church in Wales and one of the longest naves in Britain. Its 74m (242ft) nave has, in fact, been exceeded by only three other British ecclesiastical buildings – the cathedrals of York, Durham and Winchester

Atmospheric Abbey Cwmhir inspires other wistful reflections. It is reputedly the resting place of Llywelyn ap Gruffudd, Llywelyn the Last. Wales's last native prince was killed in a skirmish in 1282 at Cilmery to the south (see Builth Wells entry) and his body was brought here for burial. Although the abbey was sacked by Owain Glyndŵr in the early 15th century and demolished during the Dissolution of the Monasteries in 1536, it has not entirely disappeared. Some of its pillars were taken to the church at Llanidloes, where they can still be seen.

Abbey Cwmhir. F. Remains of once-thriving religious house in beautiful tranquil setting.

ABERAERON
DYFED   C4   *i*

Aberaeron's neat terraces and well-organized streets show unmistakable signs of an orderly approach to town planning rarely seen in Wales, where communities usually grow up higgledy-piggledy over the years. Aberaeron is different. It owes its good looks to the set plan from which it was constructed in the 19th century. Neither should we forget the vision and enterprise of 'old mad clergyman' Alban Thomas and his wife Susannah. The couple inherited a fortune, which they spent on creating, almost from scratch, a harbour and town.

Aberaeron was soon thriving as a shipbuilding centre and trading port. But the coming of the railways put an end to Cardigan Bay's great seafaring days, and Aberaeron built its last boat in 1884. Aberaeron is now a busy holiday centre. Its strongly Georgian flavour – notice how everything is designed to scale, with a clever use of repetition to create a sense of architectural harmony – can be seen to best effect along the harbour, lined with gaily painted dwellings.

Aberaeron's visitor attractions are also located around the harbour. The Tourist Information Centre is housed within a historic building, one of Aberaeron's oldest, which predates the development of the planned town. Originally a warehouse,

You can cross Aberaeron's handsome harbour by the unusual Aeron Express Aerial Ferry

it has been converted into an information centre which contains displays on the Cardigan Bay coastline.

Aberaeron's beach, mainly of pebble, stretches away from the mouth of the harbour, which is now a popular port of call with holiday sailors. A most exciting ride across the harbour is provided courtesy of the Aeron Express Aerial Ferry, an extraordinary device which whisks passengers across from quayside to quayside in a carriage worked by hand-operated pulleys.

Close by is the Aberaeron Sea Aquarium and Animal Kingdom Centre. This popular attraction contains marine exhibits, exotic live animals, displays and models. If your interest is in bees and honey, then visit the exhibition at the Hive on the Quay.

Aberaeron Sea Aquarium and Animal Kingdom Centre. Tel (0545) 570142. C. Displays of Welsh coast's marine life, tropical insects, reptiles, birds, children's corner, video.

Aeron Express Aerial Ferry. C. Re-creation of a device originally built in 1885, the first passenger-carrying ropeway in the world.

Honey Bee Exhibition, Hive on the Quay. Tel (0545) 570445. C. Observation hives of honey and bumble bees, video film. Adjoining shop sells honey products.

Nearby
Aberarth Leisure Park (1¹/₂ miles south-east of Aberaeron, on minor road off A487). Tel (0545) 570894. C. 12-hectare (30-acre) adventure and leisure park for all the family. Miniature railway, boating lake, adventure playground, tunnel maze, mini-golf, nature trail.

ABERDOVEY

GWYNEDD C3

Regular visitors to mountain-backed Aberdovey tend to be a little secretive about the place, preferring to keep its considerable charms to themselves in fear of it becoming too popular. It's easy to see why Aberdovey's devoted clientele are so protective. Firstly, it is a classy resort without the brash trappings – the bright lights, crowds and candy floss – of many places beside the sea. Secondly, it occupies an outstandingly lovely location at the mouth of the sandy Dovey estuary. And thirdly, its

The resort is a popular sailing centre

position close to the mountains of Mid Wales and the Snowdonia National Park makes it an excellent touring centre.

Many people will be familiar, if not with the resort, then with the song *Bells of Aberdovey*, composed for the late 18th-century opera *Liberty Hall*. This was inspired by the legend of a lost city, inundated by the sea, whose bells sometimes toll. The legend is the subject of a display at Aberdovey's waterfront Tourist Information Centre, which also contains exhibition panels on the resort's maritime past. By the mid-19th century, the harbourside had developed into a thriving shipping and shipbuilding centre. Slate was exported to places as far afield as Cadiz, and between 1828 and 1860 nearly 90 ships were built here.

Aberdovey's location on a narrow shelf of land backed by steep mountains has forced it to develop as a long line of buildings, with most of its hotels, self-catering accommodation, inns and shops overlooking the beach. And there's lots of beach to choose from, for the sands extend all the way from the mouth of the estuary to Tywyn. Swimming is safe if you adhere to the flag warnings and do not venture near the mouth of the estuary (there is plenty of safe water along the miles of west-facing dune-backed beach stretching to Tywyn).

The resort's sheltered waters are popular with sailing and watersports enthusiasts. Dinghy sailors will be interested to discover that the GP14 sailing dinghies were first adopted here as club boats (the black bell on the GP14's sail represents one of the 'Bells' of Aberdovey). Sailboards, dinghies and canoes are available for hire on the seafront.

Aberdovey, perched between sea and mountains

Fishermen can head for the open seas or cast their lines from the jetty; and golfers flock here to play the well-known 18-hole links course. Aberdovey is also the birthplace of the international outward bound movement, founded here in 1941.

One of the many scenic drives easily accessible from Aberdovey lies right on its doorstep. The mountain road from Cwrt (near Pennal) travels through the so-called Happy Valley (don't be put off by the meaningless name, an unfortunate Victorian appellation) to rejoin the A493 south of Tywyn. You can stop off along the way and follow a path into the hills which leads to the isolated tarn Llyn Barfog (Bearded Lake).

Outward Bound Museum (on quayside). F. Tells the story of the outward bound movement from its beginnings in Aberdovey to its international status.

ABEREDW

POWYS   **E5**

Aberedw, which sits behind a massive, protective rock outcrop, is approached by twisting roads through the lush Wye valley. Its square-towered church, St Cewydd, is tucked away from the road behind a row of cottages. Interesting features include an impressive wide porch and a 14th-century screen, and on the outside walls you can still make out ornate 18th-century memorial stones, one of which commemorates an 11-week-old baby who died in 1709. At the edge of the churchyard, just before the ground drops into a wooded valley, a stile has recently been erected into the wall in memory of an RAF pilot killed in an air crash in 1987.

CRAFTS

Corris Craft Centre

Museum of the Welsh Woollen Industry

Cambrian Factory

The silent heartlands of this unhurried, unchanging part of Wales, with its huge expanses of hill, forest and lakeland, are home to many craftspeople. Those engaged in more traditional crafts, established over generations, have been joined by forward-looking potters, ceramics and textile artists – and most welcome visitors into their workshops.

The craft most closely associated with the rural communities of old is that of the love spoon carver. Intricately shaped spoons, once used as symbols to declare love, are carved from a single piece of wood. They can still be purchased at craft shops in Mid Wales.

Celtic traditions live on in Tregaron at Rhiannon Jewellery. Here, one of the few licensed users of Welsh gold designs and makes jewellery which is inspired by Celtic legend and folklore. The jewellery has a special viewing workshop for visitors.

Much of the pleasure in visiting Wales's craft workshops comes from their surroundings, as in the case of the Marston Pottery outside Rhayader. Phil Marston, a practising potter for 15 years, has a workshop and gallery in converted 18th-century farm outbuildings. He also runs summer schools for those keen to try their hand. The Tregaron Pottery is another place that welcomes visitors who can view the processes of throwing, handling, glazing and decorating.

The tradition of woollen weaving in Wales goes back nearly 2000 years, and until the 19th century was one of the country's major industries. The weaving process is explained to visitors to the Cambrian Factory's woollen mill, Llanwrtyd Wells. The Museum of the Welsh Woollen Industry at Dre-fach Felindre near Newcastle Emlyn has an interpretive exhibition which traces wool from fleece to fabric. This site also has a working mill and a number of small craft workshops, including a papermaker where fine and decorative paper is handmade from recycled paper and plant materials.

Corris is the home of an entire crafts village, where various workshops are devoted to pottery, jewellery, leatherworking, candlemaking, toymaking, and even pyrography, the art of burning designs on wood.

Crafts are all about individual talent and skill. No two workshops are the same, as you'll discover when you delve into Mid Wales's colourful crafts scene.

Love spoons, a traditional token of betrothal in the rural Wales of bygone times

ABERGWESYN
POWYS   D4

The name Abergwesyn inspires a feeling of trepidation in the hearts of many a car rallying enthusiast. The hamlet of Abergwesyn itself – no more than a scattered collection of houses high in the Irfon valley – is not responsible for provoking such unsettling emotions. The culprit is the narrow ribbon of tarmac that winds, dips and hairpins its way westwards from the village over one of the loneliest upland areas left in southern Britain.

In the days of road rallying, the Abergwesyn Pass was *the* daunting motoring challenge, especially since it was always tackled at night. The 19th-century drovers who herded their sheep and cattle across this wilderness to markets in England must have had similar feelings about the route.

Those who do drive across the Abergwesyn Pass will travel through real, undistilled wild Welsh landscape. Fans of George Borrow's classic 19th-century travel book, *Wild Wales*, need look no further if they wish to share some of the author's experiences. He found 'some of the wildest solitudes' in these mountains, a description that still applies today. Apart from a few isolated farmsteads and one reassuring red telephone box, there is nothing in the way of civilization along the 14-mile route to Tregaron. The road initially clings to the side of a steep valley before climbing up the Devil's Staircase into a high plateau which has been variously called the 'Green Desert' or 'Roof of Wales'.

But things do change, even in remote corners of Wales. Conifer forests have now replaced much of the poor hill sheep moorland; and a new road, which allows access to the Llyn Brianne reservoir (see entry), links up with the pass. Parts of Abergwesyn's wildernesses will thankfully remain inviolate and undisturbed, for the National Trust has acquired thousands of hectares here.

There is also access off the pass to Capel Soar at Soar-y-mynydd, a remote chapel in the middle of nowhere, built to serve the thin scattering of farmsteads.

ABERGYNOLWYN
GWYNEDD   D2

This village, in the foothills of Cader Idris, has a surprisingly urban appearance. Its orderly rows of terraced dwellings were put up in the 19th century to house workers from the local slate quarry, which was developed in the 1860s and closed in 1948. Abergynolwyn's past is explained in a small village museum. The narrow-gauge Talyllyn Railway runs from Tywyn to Nant Gwernol, a wooded halt near Abergynolwyn from which a number of waymarked walks have been established.

Deeper in the hills to the north is Llanfihangel-y-pennant. Castell-y-Bere stands on the approach to this cul-de-sac village. The castle is as authentically Welsh as you can get: unlike the grand fortresses in

Lonely Castell-y-Bere in the foothills of Cader Idris

the north, built by the English invaders, Castell-y-Bere was the home of a native Welsh leader, Llywelyn ab Iorwerth, Llywelyn the Great, Prince of Gwynedd.

Mary Jones is another figure who has become part of Welsh history and folklore. In 1800, when aged 16, Mary made the 25-mile journey from Llanfihangel-y-pennant to Bala, walking barefoot for part of the way, to collect a Welsh Bible from the famous preacher, Rev Thomas Charles. Her deed is said to have inspired Charles to found the British and Foreign Bible Society. A commemorative stone to Mary stands beside the ruins of her cottage. St Michael's Church, dating from the 12th century, has a 'Leper's Window' in the north wall where those suffering from leprosy could look in to observe the service.

Follow the lovely Dysynni valley for a few miles south-west of Llanfihangel-y-pennant and you will come to a prominent 232m (761ft) outcrop known as Craig-yr-Aderyn (Bird Rock). The broad, flat valley floor was once covered by the sea; amazingly, cormorants continue to treat Bird Rock as a sea-cliff and still nest here, even though the waters of Cardigan Bay are now 4 miles away.

Nearby
Castell-y-Bere. F. Evocative ruin on a rocky outcrop. Probably built in 1221 to command what was a strategic route through the mountains (today's road lies to the south, bypassing the castle). ✿

ABERPORTH

DYFED   B5

Aberporth is one of the lesser-known delights of the Cardigan Bay coast: a tranquil seaside village where you can laze on the sands, go bathing or boating – or stride along the clifftops. It is a green and pleasant spot with a variety of copses and dingles, a fascinating blend of seaside and country. On the hillside overlooking the sandy beach there are shops, restaurants, inns and a good range of accommodation. A nearby rocket research establishment, on a headland near Aberporth, cannot be seen from the little resort and in no way diminishes the attractiveness of the area.

It's just a short walk or drive from Aberporth to cliff-backed Tre-saith

Minor roads leading off the A487 between Cardigan and Aberaeron run down to the village, which was once a busy port famed for its herring shoals. The smooth sands front a lovely inlet between two headlands. Boats can be left overnight on the beach above the high water mark and windsurfers and sea anglers find this place much to their liking. A footpath along the Ceredigion Heritage Coast, with its splendid views over the bay, runs for just over a mile eastwards to Tre-saith, a sandy beach scattered with canoes, dinghies and catamarans.

Tre-saith can also be reached by car, along the signposted minor road out of Aberporth. Just around the headland, a few minutes' drive away, is Traeth Penbryn. A 400m (¼-mile) shady walk from

the National Trust car park leads to a mainly sandy beach. One or two caves at the base of the cliffs add to the interest.

Nearby
Felinwynt Butterflies and Rain Forest Centre, Rhosmaen, Felinwynt. Tel (0239) 810882. C. An unusual attraction – exotic butterflies flying freely in a hothouse atmosphere, amid tropical plants and the taped sounds of a rain forest in Ecuador. Follow signs to Ferwig from the minor road between Blaenannerch and Aberporth.

Aberporth's sandy, sheltered beach

Take away the cars and you could almost believe that you are back in Victorian times when you stroll along Aberystwyth's wide, curving promenade. Aberystwyth's essential character, that of a Victorian seaside resort, has not been altered by the passing of the years. The 'staid respectability of its architecture', praised in one early guidebook, still sets the tone in this traditional town, which was known as the 'Biarritz' or 'Brighton of Wales' when the 19th-century railways brought holidaymakers and prosperity to Aberystwyth.

Aberystwyth lies between two hills. In the south is Pendinas, crowned by an Iron Age encampment; to the north, the promenade ends abruptly at Constitution Hill. Today, Aberystwyth fulfils at least three roles: those of a resort, university town and shopping centre. The modern university campus is spread out on the hillside overlooking a town, which by the standards of its rural neighbours, is a large and populous one, accounting for Aberystwyth's unofficial status as the 'capital' of Mid Wales.

Aberystwyth stands at the mouth of the river Rheidol. So why isn't it called Aberrheidol (aber means 'mouth of')? History provides the explanation, for this area's original Norman castle was built on the river Ystwyth a short distance to the south. Aberystwyth's surviving castle, built in 1277 to supersede the earlier stronghold put up in 1100, occupies a rock-bound headland beyond the harbour. Evidence of a hall, limekiln, bread oven and gatehouse can be seen amongst its ruins, which also contain good sections of curtain wall and ditch.

The capacious harbour

Before the coming of the railways, Aberystwyth's large, sheltered harbour was a busy port and shipbuilding centre. Hundreds of boats were constructed here, and lead and slate from mines and quarries in the mountains were brought to the harbourside for shipment.

Aberystwyth's seafaring past is recalled on headstones in St Michael's churchyard. Look out in particular for the 'Old Commodore's' gravestone in the ruined vestry (not attached to the existing

Aberystwyth is Mid Wales's unofficial 'capital'

church), which tells of the deeds of a local man who fought at the Battle of Trafalgar and 'zealously performed his duties of deputy harbourmaster at this port'.

Close to the church is Aberystwyth's original university. The seafront building housing the University of Wales Old College should never have become an academic institution. It was built in highly romantic, neo-Gothic style as a grand seaside hotel, but soon fell into financial difficulties and became instead a college. It is still part of the university, though the main campus is some distance away on Penglais hillside. This large campus contains an Arts Centre and the National Library of Wales, both of which are open to the public; there are over two million books in the library, including some of the oldest surviving manuscripts in the Welsh language and many of the greatest literary treasures of Wales and the Celtic lands.

In Aberystwyth's busy shopping streets there's the delightful Ceredigion Museum, better known locally as the Coliseum, the building's name when it served as the town's music hall and cinema. The old Edwardian theatre, with its plush, well-preserved interior, is, in many ways, the museum's prize feature. Max Miller and Gracie Fields performed in this auditorium, which is now filled with exhibits reflecting local folk history. The Tourist Information Centre is the museum's next-door neighbour.

The rural Wales of yesterday remembered within the Ceredigion Museum

Aberystwyth's distinctive period atmosphere is also reinforced by two traditional attractions on Constitution Hill. You can reach the hill's 131m (430ft) summit by the Cliff Railway, a 'conveyance of gentlefolk' since 1896. When at the summit, make the most of the panoramic views by visiting the Camera Obscura, a device whose mirror and lens system produces moving pictures of the surroundings. This new model, based on a favourite amusement of the Victorians, gazes out at over 1000 square miles of sea- and landscapes, including 26 mountain peaks

The view from the summit, unaided by Victorian technology, is spectacular enough. Below lies Aberystwyth's quarter-moon of shingle and sand

beach, a miniature of the grand, crescent-shaped sweep of Cardigan Bay. A mile to the north lies another popular beach at Clarach Bay, where a thriving seaside tourist centre has grown up around large holiday home caravan parks.

At Llanbadarn Fawr, now a suburb of Aberystwyth, there is a grand 12th-century church, one of the largest in Wales. Its size reflects the influential role which this site has played in Welsh religious affairs since the 6th century, when St Padarn founded a settlement here.

The narrow-gauge Vale of Rheidol Railway, one of Wales's 'Great Little Trains', runs from Aberystwyth to Devil's Bridge, a scenic, wooded spot deep in the hills.

Aberystwyth Arts Centre. Tel (0970) 623232 (Booking Office). F (C for performances). Galleries and exhibitions, theatre and film.

Aberystwyth Castle. F. Built by Edward I during his campaign against the Welsh. Most impressive feature is its prominent North West Gate.

Camera Obscura. Tel (0970) 617642. C. Its huge lens captures Wales from Pembrokeshire to the Llŷn peninsula.

Ceredigion Museum. Tel (0970) 617911. F. Music hall meets local history. Wide range of exhibits from the district's seafaring, farming and lead mining past.

Cliff Railway. Tel (0970) 617642. C. At 237m (778 ft) Britain's longest electric-powered cliff railway. Climbs Constitution Hill's 2-in-1 gradient at a sedate 4mph.

Vale of Rheidol Railway. Tel Brecon Mountain Railway (0685) 4854 for information. C. Chuffs through beautiful Rheidol valley for 12 miles to Devil's Bridge.

Nearby
Rheidol Hydro-electric Scheme, Cwm Rheidol (off A44 at Capel Bangor). Tel (097084) 667. C. Tours of environment-friendly power station and fish farm in beautiful secluded setting. Nature trail, fishing, waterfalls, floodlit weir.

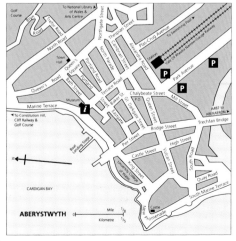

MARKET DAYS

The country comes to town on market day. If you want to experience the bustle and atmosphere of a Welsh market, then plan your visit from the list below. Market days are great social as well as commercial occasions – it's the day in the week when farming folk not only buy and sell livestock, but also catch up on the local gossip.

Cattle sales at Tregaron

LIVESTOCK MARKETS

Aberystwyth	Monday (fortnightly)
Bala	Thursday (weekly)
Builth Wells	Monday (weekly)
Caersws	Saturday (fortnightly & seasonal)
Cardigan	Monday (weekly)
Cemmaes Road	Thursday (weekly)
Dolgellau	Friday (weekly)
Knighton	Thursday & Friday (weekly)
Lampeter	Monday (fortnightly)
Llanfair Caereinion	Tuesday (weekly & seasonal)
Llanidloes	Saturday (fortnightly & seasonal)
Llanwrtyd Wells	Thursday (fortnightly & seasonal)
Llanybydder	Monday (fortnightly); Horse sales last Thursday every month
Machynlleth	Wednesday (weekly)
Newcastle Emlyn	Friday (weekly)
Newtown	Thursday (fortnightly)
Rhayader	Wednesday (weekly)
Tregaron	Tuesday (fortnightly)
Welshpool	Monday (weekly)

GENERAL MARKETS

There are also many weekly general markets held throughout Mid Wales, where stallholders set up shop either under cover or in the streets. Some coincide with livestock markets.

Aberystwyth	Monday
Barmouth	Thursday
Builth Wells	Monday & Friday
Cardigan	Saturday & Monday
Lampeter	Alternate Tuesdays
Llanidloes	Saturday
Machynlleth	Wednesday
Newcastle Emlyn	Friday
Newtown	Tuesday & Saturday
Rhayader	Wednesday

Wales is an eventful country. A full and lively programme of events takes place throughout the year – there's everything from music festivals to medieval pageants, guided walks to country fairs. In a guide of this size, it's impossible to mention them all, or to give specific dates. Please call in at a Tourist Information Centre for the full picture.

We have made brief reference to selected important events under the relevant locations in the gazetteer. Wales's three major annual events are the Llangollen International Musical Eisteddfod, which takes place in North Wales for a week in the first part of July, the Royal Welsh Agricultural Show, held in Builth Wells, Mid Wales, for four days in late July, and the week-long Royal National Eisteddfod, held at a different location each year in the first part of August.

A prize exhibit at the Royal Welsh Agricultural Show

Bala Lake

Bala stands at the eastern end of 4-mile-long Llyn Tegid (Bala Lake), the largest natural lake in Wales. The town, which basically consists of one long, tree-lined main street of shops, inns and eating places, is traditionally Welsh in tone and temperament. The scene is set by a statue of the Liberal MP and advocate of home rule for Wales, Thomas Edward Ellis (1859–99), in suitably flamboyant pose.

Bala's strong associations with Wales's cultural and religious traditions include its links with the Rev Thomas Charles (1755–1814). There is a memorial plaque above the former home (now Barclays Bank) of this inspirational leader of Welsh Nonconformism and the Sunday School movement, who preached to packed congregations wherever he went. Another plaque is dedicated to Mary Jones, a 16-year-old who walked 25 miles to Bala from Llanfihangel-y-pennant (see Abergynolwyn entry), barefoot part of the way, to ask Charles for a Bible.

The town has grown up around an earthwork, Tomen y Bala, possibly of Norman or even Iron Age origin. Its wooded mound, surrounded by houses, now looks comically out of place. Bala is a magnificent touring centre for Snowdonia and Mid Wales. Its lake occupies a natural fault between the Aran and Arennig mountains. Fishing and watersports are excellent, though anglers will be lucky to catch the elusive gwyniad, a white fish of the salmon species which hides in its deep waters and is reputedly unique to the lake.

The Bala Adventure and Watersports Centre, between the lake and the banks of the river Tryweryn, offers facilities, courses and activities; the National White Water Centre has a full programme of canoeing events on the river Tryweryn

A one-hour trip along the shore of Bala Lake can be made on a narrow-gauge railway which travels between Bala and Llanuwchllyn (see Llanuwchllyn entry).

Spectacular mountain roads lead south and north from Bala through lonely upland wildernesses (take the road to mountain-locked Lake Vyrnwy, for example, and complete the circular tour by returning along Bwlch y Groes, the highest road in Wales).

Bala Lake Railway. Tel (06784) 666. C. Lakeside narrow-gauge line. One of the 'Great Little Trains of Wales'. Main terminus at nearby Llanuwchllyn.

Barmouth can be enjoyed on more than one level – literally. On the one hand, it's a popular resort with all that the description implies – miles of firm, clean sands, a picturesque harbour, a variety of amusements and something for all the family. On the other, it's an architectural oddity – a town that climbs a hillside so precipitously that on the upper levels the houses seem to be perched on each other's rooftops.

Either way, Barmouth is a delight. It stands where the Mawddach estuary flows into the sea, and the views across the waters are ever-changing and memorable. The town has a proud maritime history and this is reflected in the little quayside museum marking the deeds of local lifeboatmen. Nearby is Tŷ Gwyn, where Harri Tudur's (Henry Tudor's) campaign against Richard III was reputedly planned

Buckets and spades and beautiful coastal scenery come together at popular Barmouth

15

A walk with a difference, across the railway bridge which spans the mouth of the Mawddach at Barmouth

by his uncle – who thus helped to make him Henry VII after the Battle of Bosworth in 1485.

A town trail runs from St John's Church – unmistakable for its size and for the gilt clock in its tower – to the viewpoint of Dinas Oleu, which has an important place in the history of conservation in Britain as the first piece of land ever to be acquired by the National Trust. The trail involves a stiff climb, but those who make it are rewarded with panoramic views of Cardigan Bay and the Cader Idris range. St David's Church in the town centre is notable for its eight rare copies of cartoons by Raphael. Behind the church a fascinating maze of steep lanes climbs up the hillside.

There are plenty of sights at ground level too, including that of the 730m ('/2-mile) part-timber railway bridge, bravely flung across the estuary in 1867. There is a pedestrian walkway the length of the bridge, which is part of the Cambrian Coast Railway, one of British Rail's most scenic lines. The narrow-gauge line across the estuary, known as the Fairbourne and Barmouth Steam Railway, has connections with Barmouth via a ferry service (see Fairbourne entry).

Llanaber Church, a mile or so north of Barmouth on the A496, contains the Calixtus Stone from the Dark Ages, with an inscription that defies scholars. The church's clerestory is recognized as a beautiful example of the Early English style.

Barmouth Leisure Centre. Tel (0341) 280111. C. New centre with sports facilities and children's activities.

Lifeboat Museum. F. Unusual attraction run by the Royal National Lifeboat Institution. Photographs of old lifeboats and lifeboatmen, models of sailing ships, certificates for heroism.

Tŷ Crwn. F. Old lock-up near harbour now housing exhibition of finds from two wrecks 400m ('/4 mile) off coast by local divers. Spanish and French coins, bronze bell dated 1677, cannon balls, pewter plates.

Tŷ Gwyn. F. More finds from shipwrecks and medieval exhibition in this historic old building overlooking harbour.

BERRIEW

POWYS **F2**

The border village of Berriew, past winner of the 'Best Kept Village in Wales' award, is a picturesque place with fine examples of the black-and-white half-timbered cottages common to these parts. Many of these old houses were built in Tudor and Stuart times, when the village prospered as a wool-trading centre.

The village's architectural beauty blends in well with its lovely surroundings, on the banks of the river Rhiw amongst rolling, wooded hills.

BORTH

DYFED **C3**

Three miles of sand attract many families to Borth, a resort midway along Cardigan Bay. There's everything here from rock pools (under the cliffs) to sand dunes (at Ynyslas – see separate entry), safe swimming on Borth's gently shelving beach (especially suitable for young children) to sailing and watersports (this is good sailboarding territory). The village, strung out beside this beach in a long line of cafés, shops, amusements and places to stay, is the only one in Britain to be built on a shingle bank. There's excellent golf at Borth's long-established 18-hole links course.

For the best view of Borth and its uncharacteristically flat surroundings, go to the rocky headland at Upper Borth and gaze northwards towards the mountain-backed Dovey estuary.

Borth Animalarium. Tel (0970) 871224. C. A wide range of animals, from goats to tarantulas, which can be viewed largely under cover. Lots of friendly animals to stroke.

Borth's long beach extends all the way to the mouth of the Dovey estuary

POWYS   E4

Builth Wells is anything but a static place. The jumble of architectural styles which crowds its narrow streets bears witness to a lively past. Since its 11th-century beginnings around a Norman castle (now reduced to earthworks), this solid market town has played many roles. It was near here that the course of Welsh history was decided when Llywelyn ap Gruffudd, Llywelyn the Last, was killed by English soldiers in 1282. The death of the last native Welsh prince destroyed any hopes of national unity and allowed Edward I to complete his conquest. A memorial stone at Cilmery, about 4 miles west of Builth, recalls the prince's fate.

The entertainment-packed Royal Welsh Show

colourful gathering takes place in late July in the Llanelwedd Showground, just across the handsome bridge which spans the river Wye.

As if to emphasize Builth's modern image, the 1870s Assembly Room on the riverbank has been turned into the Wyeside Arts Centre, where there is a wide range of entertainment on hand. The town's emblem of a white ox is pictured in relief on the building's façade.

On the hill above the river and car park there are plenty of interesting shops and cafés selling home-made food; and a walk into the mountains which surround the town (use a good map) will reward you with appealing views of the Wye and Irfon valleys.

Wyeside Arts Centre. Tel (0982) 552555. F (C for performances). Cinema, restaurant, theatre and gallery with changing exhibitions.

A picnic beside the river Wye at Builth

In the 17th century, discontent focused on religious issues and reformer John Wesley was an occasional guest preacher at St Mary's Church in the middle of town (Llanfair-ym-Muallt, the town's Welsh name, means 'The Church in the Cow Pasture'). The 14th-century church tower still stands, alongside a Victorian extension, and you can see the outline of the original church roof. A worn stone effigy of a Tudor gentleman lies in the porchway; his ruff and moustache are still discernable, and a dog lies at his feet.

It was in the Victorian age of touring gentlefolk that Llanfair-ym-Muallt became Builth Wells. Saline water was first discovered here in 1830, and by the late 19th century the town's central Pavilion was kept busy by visitors eager to cure their ills by taking the waters'. Nowadays Builth has shaken off its Victorian gentility, though many sturdy buildings of that era remain. Its modern claim to fame is as the host town of the annual Royal Welsh Agricultural Show. This major four-day event – featuring displays of machinery, animals and crafts, together with much in the way of general entertainment – draws vast crowds from farming and non-farming areas and is a major televised event in Wales. This

CAERSWS

POWYS   E3

Travellers have been passing through Caersws for many centuries. The main railway line to Shrewsbury and London from the Cambrian coast runs through this sprawling village, as well as the main road from South to North Wales. Nearly 2000 years ago the Romans had already recognized its strategic position at the confluence of the Severn, Garno and Trannon rivers. A Roman road was built through Caersws, linking the major eastern garrisons with their western outposts. Two forts have been discovered in the area, one dating from the 1st century AD, and excavations have revealed that a Roman village grew up around the stationed garrisons. Between Caersws and Llandinam, oval banks of earth mark the outline of Cefn Carnedd Celtic hillfort, where Prince Caratacus (Caradog) is said to have made his last stand against the Romans.

On the outskirts of the village are the austere brick buildings of Llys Maldwyn – now a hospital, but originally the 19th-century workhouse.

Frustrated rally drivers can try the real thing at a 'Forest Experience' rally school at nearby Carno.

CARDIGAN
DYFED B5

St Dogmael's Abbey

Cardigan is a bright and bustling market town with lots of character. It was once one of the principal ports along the west coast of Wales and although its days of maritime glory are over, much of interest remains. The long main street is remarkable for the variety of its shops and hotels, some of the inns going back to the days of the stagecoach.

Cardigan was granted a royal charter in 1230, but its story begins well before that. This was part of the hotly contested territory of Deheubarth in the days when the Norman invaders came up against the stubborn Welsh princes. The remains of the castle, overlooking the centuries-old stone bridge across the Teifi at the southern approach to the town, are visible proof of the power struggles of that far-distant time. The castle changed hands frequently in the 12th century but was certainly held by the Welsh in 1176, as the powerful Lord Rhys staged the first eisteddfod there.

The lovely Cenarth Falls

One of the town's architectural jewels is the old Guildhall, with its arches and clock tower. It is no longer an administrative centre but houses a fascinating array of market stalls, some of which sell local produce. Geoffrey Powell's beautiful sculpture of a Teifi otter, on the town side of the bridge, was presented to Cardigan by David Bellamy. The Cardigan Wildlife Park is located a few miles to the south (see Cilgerran entry).

Cardigan Castle. Scanty remains of a circular keep and two towers. Interior not open to public. View from outside only.

Theatr Mwldan. Tel (0239) 612687. Community theatre with lively range of productions.

Nearby
St Dogmael's Abbey. F. Remains of 12th-century Benedictine abbey attractively sited on hillside. Epitaphs to shipwrecked mariners in adjacent churchyard. Signposted road from St Dogmael's village to nearby Poppit Sands. ✪

Y Felin, St Dogmael's. Tel (0239) 613999. C. Working watermill producing stoneground flour, opposite abbey. Duckpond at roadside.

CENARTH
DYFED B5

This tiny village was immortalized by the 12th-century traveller Gerald of Wales (Giraldus Cambrensis), who wrote of the salmon leaping there 'as high as the tallest spear'. There were beavers in the river Teifi then, but you won't find any now.

The flat rocks exposed when the water is low are handy platforms for viewing Cenarth Falls – a much-visited beauty spot since Victorian times – where the Teifi spumes in a series of small descents. Cenarth's handsome three-arch bridge goes back two centuries. St Llawddog's Church has beautiful stained glass and a 5th-century stone in the

18

churchyard, near the porch, with a Latin inscription: *Curcagn-i Fili Andagell* (Curcagnus, son of Andagellus).

Cenarth's working watermill also serves as an interpretive centre where various kinds of coracle – a small one-man boat with a basketwork frame which goes back to pre-Roman times – are on display. The mill is also the location of a coraclemaker's workshop. Visitors to Cenarth can sometimes see coracles in action on the waters of the Teifi.

Cenarth Mill and Coracle Centre. Tel (0239) 710209. Mill F. Coracle Centre C. 17th-century flour mill. Old photographs of coracle fishermen, as well as examples of different kinds of coracle. More ambitious coracle centre in course of development.

Nearby
Fferm Glyneithinog, Penrherber. Tel (0239) 710432. F. Watch the cheesemaking on certain days – check before going.

Coracle fishing on the Teifi

CILGERRAN
DYFED   B5

This trim village in the Teifi valley is justly famed for its castle, which stands on a crag high above the river. Lovers of the romantic relish the tale of how the Welsh Helen', Nest – wife of the Norman overlord – was abducted here by a Welsh prince in 1109. The present castle dates from 1223. Its twin towers still have a swaggering and domineering look. Steep flights of stone steps enable the visitor to see their interior.

Coracle fishermen may sometimes be seen in the vicinity and there is a Coracle Regatta every August.

Cardigan Wildlife Park (on western approach to Cilgerran). Tel (0239) 614449. C. Attractive 20-hectare (50-acre) park with red deer, polecats, minx, Shetland and Exmoor ponies – and Iron Age pigs!

Cilgerran Castle, on a wooded bluff above the river

Cilgerran Castle. Tel (0239) 615136. C. Key to padlocked gate obtainable from nearby shop.

Nearby
Bro-Meigan Gardens and Tea Rooms, Boncath. Tel (0239) 841232. C. 2¹/₂ hectares (6 acres) of formal gardens, varied and attractively landscaped, created out of former smallholding. Marvellous views towards Mynydd Preseli.

CLYRO
POWYS   F5

There are two good reasons to visit Clyro: its wide views of the rolling border hills, and its links with 19th-century diarist Francis Kilvert. Kilvert was Clyro's curate in the 1860s and '70s, living in Ash Brook House. His descriptions of the Marcher country and its people met with huge success when they were published in the 1930s. A stone in the pleasant, airy church commemorates Kilvert's association with the village, and a small display matches names on the parish records with snippets of their day-to-day life from the diaries. The church is worth exploring for its interesting memorial tablets, including one to the Archdeacon of Brecon, Edward Edwards, who died in 1803 and is remembered for his 'amiable disposition and polished manners'.

Kilvert is also recalled on a commemorative sundial at Llowes churchyard, a few miles south-west of Clyro on the A438. Inside the homely little church, St Meilig's, stands a stone Celtic cross which dates back to about AD600. The cross's original site was on the mountain at Croes Feilig (Meilig's Cross), but it was moved to the churchyard in the 12th century and into the church itself in 1956, where its bold and simple Celtic design can still be admired.

Maesyronnen Chapel is set on a steep hillside, ¹/₂ mile off the A438 near Glasbury. This long, low chapel, which overlooks the river Llynfi and the Black Mountains, was founded in 1696 and is one of the oldest Nonconformist meeting-houses in Wales. If you want to take a look inside, call in at the Old Post Office, Ffynnon Gynydd, for the keys.

Nearby
Maesyronnen Chapel (off A438 between Glasbury and Llowes). F. Wales's first chapel?

Cader Idris

Bala Lake

It's a big mistake to think that the Snowdonia National Park is confined to North Wales. Although the park is named after the mountain of Snowdon in the north, most of its land mass – over 500 of its 840 square miles – is located in Mid Wales.

This part of Snowdonia boasts one of the last true areas of wilderness left in southern Britain. The Rhinogs, inland from Harlech, are an empty, inhospitable upland mass of heather moorland and exposed rocks which roads have yet to penetrate.

The park extends southwards all the way to Machynlleth, encompassing a huge swathe of uplands. The mountains of Mid Wales are subtly different to those in the north. The severe, serrated skyline of Snowdonia's rocky, northern reaches is replaced with greener, more rounded profiles further south. The Aran and Arennig mountains around Bala, for example, rise like giant, green waves from the valley floor. Statistically, the mountains of southern Snowdonia fail to reach the heights of their northern neighbours, falling short of the magic 1000m (3281ft) mark (Cader Idris, the highest mountain in Mid Wales, stands at 892m/2927ft, compared with Snowdon's 1085m/3560ft). In practice, the difference is an academic one, for Mid Wales's highlands are as challenging – and should be treated with the same respect – as the north's peaks.

Overlooking Dolgellau is brooding Cader Idris, a formidable mountain whose screes, ridges and summit are as powerful as they come. Cader Idris's massive bulk is made even more emphatic because of its close proximity to the sea; and seashore is another ingredient which adds to the variety to be found within the Snowdonia National Park. The northern shores of Cardigan Bay, from Aberdovey to Harlech, form the western boundary of the park. This 30-mile mountain-backed coastline contains dunes, beaches and two outstandingly beautiful estuaries, created by the Mawddach and Dovey rivers.

Information centres located at Aberdovey, Bala, Dolgellau and Harlech will be happy to supply further details on all aspects of the Snowdonia National Park.

The Mawddach estuary, a luxuriant blend of sand, sea, woodland and mountain

CORRIS
GWYNEDD   D2

Call in at the Corris Craft Centre

Some visitors find Corris, a village of narrow streets and dark-stoned terraces topped with the inevitable slate roofs, a little off-putting; others are intrigued by this little community hemmed in by thick forests and steep mountain slopes. Slate is the key to Corris's past. The village grew up alongside its slate quarries, which flourished in the second half of the 19th century when 1000 men were employed here. Such was the size of the enterprise that the community spilled over into two villages, Corris and Corris Uchaf (Upper Corris).

Life in Corris in its heyday must have been like living on the platform of Paddington Station. Narrow-gauge trains rattled through the cramped streets right past the doorsteps on their way from the quarries to Machynlleth. The village boasted one of the most impressive narrow-gauge stations in Britain. The story of the railway, which closed in 1948, is told at the Corris Railway Museum.

Corris looks to the future as well as the past. The modernistic Corris Craft Centre stands beside the A487. This purpose-built complex of attractively designed units contains a variety of workshops, a Tourist Information Centre and children's adventure playground.

Corris Craft Centre. Tel (0654) 761244. F. Craftspeople with many different skills at work. A good stopping-off place.

Corris Railway Museum. F. Charming little museum full of the clutter of the Corris Railway. Old photographs, historical displays. Run by the Corris Railway Society, who are restoring part of the old line.

CREGENNEN LAKES
GWYNEDD   C2

Take the minor road from Dolgellau that climbs along the northern shoulder of Cader Idris and within 5 miles you'll come to the lovely Cregennen Lakes. This pair of lakes lie in glorious open countryside, poised between the bare escarpments of Cader Idris and the luxuriant Mawddach estuary.

The views from this lofty spot are magnificent. The most direct – and scenic – approach to the lakes is along the winding road from Arthog on the banks of the estuary, which climbs abruptly from sea level to nearly 300m (over 900ft). If you have time to take your eyes off the road you'll enjoy panoramic views of the mouth of the Mawddach and the resort of Barmouth, looking like a toy-town built at its sandy entrance.

Despite their relatively obscure location, more and more visitors are now discovering the Cregennen Lakes; so it is fortuitous that they are in the care of the National Trust, who will no doubt guard against any unsympathetic development at this beautiful spot.

The Cregennen Lakes, high in the mountains

The falls at Devil's Bridge, in their spectacular 'dread chasm'

CWM YSTWYTH

DYFED **D4**

Approaching the hamlet of Cwm Ystwyth from the east along the mountain road from Rhayader, you'll suddenly enter a strange, lunar-like world of spoil heaps, industrial debris and abandoned mineworkings. These ghostly workings are the remnants of Cwm Ystwyth's lead mine – one of the largest in Mid Wales – which reached its peak of production in the 17th and 18th centuries. The shells of workers' dwellings stand close to an extensive complex of decaying mine buildings. The mine closed in 1916 and it doesn't look as if anyone has been near the place since – so don't be tempted to take a closer look for yourself, but instead view this precarious site from the roadside.

This encounter with Cwm Ystwyth's industrial past seems all the more alien since the mine is situated amongst mountains and moorlands that have changed little over the centuries, and today still cling to their hill sheep farming traditions. You'll need to watch out for the dozy sheep as you drive across the spectacular mountain road which climbs up from Rhayader to a bleakly beautiful moorland plateau before descending into the steep-sided valley carved by the infant river Ystwyth.

DEVIL'S BRIDGE

DYFED **D3**

It has become a bit of a cliché to remark that the first thing you'll see at Devil's Bridge is a clutch of puzzled visitors asking 'Where the devil is the bridge?' Profuse woodlands and a gloomy gorge conspire to hide the old bridges – for there are more than one – from view.

Three bridges in all, stacked one above the next, span the narrow 91m- (300ft-) deep chasm carved by the river Mynach. Beginning at the top we have the 'modern' road bridge, built of iron in 1901. Beneath lies a stone bridge put up in 1753, which stands above the original Pont-y-gwr-Drwg (The Bridge of the Evil Man), built by Cistercian monks in the 12th century. It is this early bridge which is associated with the devilish legend. The Devil is said to have built it so that an old woman could cross the gorge to retrieve her cow, on condition that he would own the first living creature to use the bridge. On its completion, he beckoned to the woman to cross, but she outwitted him by throwing a crust of bread over the bridge which her dog chased. So the Devil kept the dog instead of the woman.

There is a viewing platform below the three bridges, from which you can also see the so-called

'Devil's Punch Bowl', where the swirling Mynach has gouged strange shapes into the rocks before plunging over magnificent falls. These waterfalls are best seen by following a path which drops into the depths of the wooded chasm via a series of steps, including 'Jacob's Ladder', an unbroken staircase of 100 steps. Just after the falls, the Mynach joins the river Rheidol. If one waterfall is not enough for you, then you can also visit the Gyfarllwyd Falls a little way upstream on the river Rheidol.

Visitors have been attracted to Devil's Bridge for centuries. Following a visit to this 'dread chasm' in 1824, William Wordsworth felt compelled to write one of his celebrated sonnets. George Borrow, whose travel book *Wild Wales* is a 19th-century classic, described the place as 'one of the most remarkable locations in the world'.

By the early 1900s, with the opening of the narrow-gauge railway from Aberystwyth, people were coming here by the trainload. Steam-powered engines continue to puff laboriously up the scenic 12-mile route through the Vale of Rheidol.

A mile or so south-eastwards from the village, the B4574 crests a 373m (1223ft) summit marked by a rough stone arch. This monument was erected by landowner Thomas Johnes in 1810 to commemorate the jubilee of King George III. Johnes devoted much of his life to a worthy, but overambitious, attempt to transform his Hafod estate through the infusion of money, new farming methods, learning and culture (he is said to have planted six million trees as part of his grand plan!). His house, popularized in

You can reach Devil's Bridge by narrow-gauge railway

the book *Peacocks in Paradise* by Elisabeth Inglis-Jones, was finally demolished in 1962 (see Pontrhydygroes entry).

Mynach Falls. C. Follow a steep path down into the chasm for spectacular views of the falls.

Vale of Rheidol Railway. Te! Brecon Mountain Railway (0685) 4854 for information. C. One of Wales's 'Great Little Trains'. Travels to Devil's Bridge from its main terminus at Aberystwyth.

DINAS MAWDDWY

GWYNEDD   D2

Weaving at the Meirion Mill

Dinas Mawddwy was an important market town at one time, with claims to a 14th-century charter, but it is now no more – and no less – than a highly picturesque village, just off the A470 between Mallwyd and Dolgellau. It has a historic inn bilingually named the Llew Coch/Red Lion, and a few doors away a stone cottage serves as the local branch of the Midland Bank.

The old-world atmosphere owes much to the fact that the main road bypasses the village, which is encircled by steep-sided, wooded mountains. The lofty Bwlch y Groes mountain road, at 546m (1791ft) the highest road in Wales, claws its way over remote uplands north-east of Dinas Mawddwy towards Llanuwchllyn and Bala.

Meirion Mill. Tel (06504) 311. F. Weaving unit and mill shop with tweeds, tapestries, rugs, coats and other products. Mill was once terminus for now defunct Mawddwy Railway. Don't miss Pont Minllyn, just inside entrance to mill complex, a grass-topped packhorse bridge built in 17th century by local rector.

DOLGELLAU

GWYNEDD   D2

Dolgellau is a town which inspires strong opinions amongst its visitors. There are those who are enchanted by its dark-stoned streets, which seem to spring up naturally from their setting in the shadows of the mighty Cader Idris mountain. Others find Dolgellau's architecture too sombre for their tastes, especially when the rain brings an extra pitch of blackness to the local stone and slate.

Whatever your feelings, you'll have to admit that Dolgellau is different. There are not many places which display such rigid architectural uniformity. Dolgellau's restrained, robust buildings are almost entirely made of the same dark boulder stone and lighter granite, which, from a distance, give the impression that the whole town has been carved from a single block of material.

Stone-built Dolgellau is surrounded by some of Mid Wales's finest mountain scenery

Dolgellau stands beside the rivermeadows of the Wnion valley surrounded by the mountains of the Snowdonia National Park. It is one of the best-located touring centres in Wales, being within easy driving distance of the northern peaks, the Mid Wales heartlands and the Cardigan Bay coast. Dolgellau is also an important meeting place. Livestock markets have been held here for centuries, and in its time Dolgellau has been a centre for the wool trade, tanning, knitting and even gold prospecting (this precious metal, found in the local rocks, inspired a mini-gold rush in the 19th century when staid Dolgellau became Wales's answer to the Klondike). Market day is Friday.

The town's narrow streets and shady nooks and crannies are full of interesting buildings. Glyndŵr Street is named after Owain Glyndŵr, the folk-hero who held a Welsh parliament here in the early 15th-century uprising against English rule. Nearby is St Mary's Church, whose fine interior contains exceptional 18th- and 19th-century stained-glass windows and a magnificent roof supported by rows of hefty wooden pillars.

Cymer Abbey

Eldon Square, in the heart of the town, is the only place where Dolgellau's narrow passageways loosen their grip. This airy, open area is the home of a museum whose contents reflect the strong links which this part of Wales has with the Quaker movement, and the Quakers' emigration to America. A long-established, twice-yearly fair is held here in late April and late September.

Llanelltyd, a mile or so to the north-west, is the home of two interesting religious sites. Cymer Abbey, beautifully located beside the river Mawddach, was founded by Cistercian monks in 1198. It never achieved the prosperity of other Cistercian houses in Wales, though its ruins do contain evidence of architectural finesse, most notably in the three arched windows in the east wall and the craftsmanship of the surviving columns. On the opposite side of the river is St Illtyd's Church, one of the few in Britain with a circular churchyard. This ancient church contains a stone into which has been carved a footprint and 9th- or 10th-century lettering which means, 'The footprint of Kenyric (a pilgrim) is imprinted at the head of this stone before he himself set out for foreign parts.'

Walkers are spoilt for choice in this area. The famous Torrent Walk, 2 miles east of Dolgellau, follows the banks of the Clywedog as it tumbles down a steep, wooded valley. The Precipice Walk in the hills to the north-east is even better. This spectacular path runs along the lake of Llyn Cynwch before clinging to a high, steep-sided ridge above the Mawddach from which there are glorious views of the lovely estuary in its mountainous setting.

If that seems all too tame for you, then head into the misty heights of 892m (2927ft) Cader Idris, a looming mountain which guards the southern gateway to the Snowdonia National Park. The mountain – which means 'The Chair of Idris' – was named after a mythical giant and warrior. According to legend, anyone who spends a night on its rocky summit will awake either a poet or a madman – or not at all. This is serious, challenging walking country, so make sure that you are well-prepared if you intend clambering to the summit (the Minffordd Path is a good route – see Tal-y-llyn Lake entry).

In the hills above Bontddu, along the northern shores of the Mawddach estuary, are the mines that supplied gold for a number of royal wedding rings.

Museum of the Quakers. Tel (0341) 422341 Meirionnydd District Council for information. F. Exhibits on area's links with Quaker movement and emigration.

Nearby
Cymer Abbey, Llanelltyd. Tel (0341) 422854. C. Remains of a simple abbey, founded in late 12th century by Cistercian monks. ✣

DOL-GOCH
GWYNEDD   C2

The best way to arrive at this pretty place is by narrow-gauge railway. The Talyllyn Railway (see Tywyn entry) stops here so that passengers can visit the Dol-goch Falls. Paths lead from the halt to a series of waterfalls in a deep, wooded glen, which was given as a gift to the people of Tywyn by a local benefactor. Dol-goch is also easily reached by road.

DYFFRYN ARDUDWY
GWYNEDD   C2

Handsome stone houses line the road in this small village overlooking the dunes that fringe the beach 800m (¹/₂ mile) to the west. An unusual cromlech with two burial chambers can be reached by way of a signposted path at the southern end of the village. This entails a short walk up a gentle slope. The site commands a sweeping view across Tremadog Bay to the Llŷn peninsula.

Dyffryn Ardudwy Burial Chamber. F. Neolithic (New Stone Age) tomb with two distinct chambers 9m (30ft) apart, built at different times – western chamber came first. Stones from mound once covering this tomb lie scattered around. ✣

DYLIFE
POWYS   D3

If you're a fan of high, wild, lonely places, then you won't want to miss Dylife. This scattered hamlet stands, exposed to the elements, on the mountain road halfway between Llanidloes and Machynlleth. Despite its remote location, Dylife was not immune to the heavy hand of industry. Mountain moorland has been scoured away or buried beneath grey lead waste from a large mine which operated here from the 1770s to 1896.

Nature soon reasserts itself outside Dylife. On its eastern approach is Ffrwd Fawr, a waterfall created by the river Twymyn as it plunges suddenly down a steep valley hidden from view below the road.

Head north-westwards from Dylife and you'll cross one of Wales's most memorable mountain roads. The road climbs to a high point of 509m (1671ft), at which you feel as though you are on top of the world as a stunning panorama of mountain peaks unfolds before you. A short distance from the summit, in the direction of Machynlleth, look out for a viewpoint carved in dark slate. The writer and broadcaster Wynford Vaughan-Thomas (1908–87) has been honoured by a memorial, unveiled in 1990, which must be the finest roadside viewpoint in Wales. Jointly erected by the Council for the Protection of Rural Wales, the British Broadcasting Company and Harlech Television, the beautifully carved memorial identifies the Welsh peaks which can be seen from this commanding spot.

At the road's high point, you can follow a rough track for a mile or so to the remote mountain lake of Glaslyn. There is a circular walk around the lake, which is part of the 216-hectare (535-acre) Glaslyn Nature Reserve, a wilderness area of heather moorland, bog, rough grassland and ravine.

The splendid viewpoint on the Dylife mountain road is dedicated to broadcaster Wynford Vaughan-Thomas

Dyffryn Ardudwy's prehistoric burial chamber

The archway at remote Strata Florida Abbey

Mountain-locked Castell-y-Bere

Ever since the coming of the Romans to Britain's shores 2000 years ago, Mid Wales's remote hills and mountains have served as a refuge from invading forces. The relative scarcity of large camps and castles in this part of Wales is indicative of an area which remained untamed by Roman generals and Norman warlords.

In earlier times, parts of Mid Wales were settled by prehistoric man. At Dyffryn Ardudwy, Stone Age tribes built a burial chamber which survives to this day. The site known as Muriau'r Gwyddelod, a little further north near Harlech, has the well-preserved foundations of Iron Age huts. Many a Mid Wales hilltop is crowned by an Iron Age fort. Pendinas, the prominent summit south of Aberystwyth, and Ffridd Faldwyn, the spur above Montgomery, are two such fortifications.

The earthen barrier known as Offa's Dyke dates from the 8th century. Some of the best-preserved sections of this ditch and mound – the first official border between England and Wales – can be seen in the hills around Knighton.

Mid Wales's silent hills were a retreat for religious men. Cistercian monks established a medieval settlement at Strata Florida, near Pontrhydfendigaid, which became the 'Westminster Abbey of Wales'. The Cistercians also founded Abbey Cwmhir, north of Llandrindod Wells, and Cymer Abbey, near Dolgellau.

Military men usually gave Mid Wales's wildernesses a wide berth, yet the region boasts one of Europe's finest medieval castles. Mighty Harlech stands on a craggy outcrop overlooking mountain and sea, its authoritative presence undimmed by the passage of time. Harlech was built in the 13th century by the English king Edward I as part of his master plan to subdue the Welsh. Castell-y-Bere, near Abergynolwyn, represents the other side of the coin: a mountain stronghold of the Welsh native princes. Welshpool's Powis Castle is yet another breed. This grand mansion, surrounded by beautiful parklands and gardens, began life as a humble border fortress.

Although the Industrial Revolution touched this region only lightly, Mid Wales's green hills were mined for lead, silver and gold. The Llywernog Silver-Lead Mining Museum near Ponterwyd and the Bryntail Lead Mine at Llyn Clywedog are two places which preserve memories of Mid Wales's industrial heritage.

Llywernog Silver-Lead Mining Museum

Craig-goch dam

ELAN VALLEY

POWYS **E4**

The Elan valley lakelands are the first and most famous of Mid Wales's many man-made reservoirs. They were built between 1892 and 1903 to supply water to the city of Birmingham, 73 miles away. Their construction also had another effect: coachloads of visitors began to arrive, putting nearby Rhayader on the tourist map and creating an identity for the 'Mid Wales lakelands' which has since been strengthened by the creation of further reservoirs throughout the region.

But you can't beat the original. The Elan valley lakes, despite the stiff competition, remain the firm favourites. The valley's four lakes are the most scenic reservoirs in Mid Wales, probably because they have had plenty of time to settle in amongst the folds of the mountains. Their attractiveness is also due to the style in which their dams were built with blocks of dressed stone, together with the occasional architectural flourish and decorative feature missing from their plainer, more functional modern counterparts.

Your first port of call should be the Elan Valley Visitor Centre, located beneath the Caban-coch dam and close to the delightful 'model' village of Elan built in 1906–9 to house waterworks staff. Exhibitions within tell the story of farming, wildlife, water supply and times gone by. The lakes form the basis of a 18,207-hectare (45,000-acre) estate, an area renowned not only for the natural beauty of its open mountains, moors and oakwoods but also for its prolific birdlife (it is the best inland site in Wales for birds and the home of the rare red kite). An active ranger service is based at the centre, providing visitors with a programme of guided walks and talks as well as being involved in everything from waymarking footpaths to the protection of rare birds. Outside, overlooking the river Elan, is a statue of the poet Shelley (1792–1822), who lived with his first wife in a house now

submerged beneath the waters of Caban-coch. When the reservoirs were constructed, 18 farm-houses, a school and a church were destroyed.

Driving northwards from Caban-coch you'll come next to the Garreg-ddu reservoir, followed by Pen-y-garreg and Craig-goch, four reservoirs in all which form a snaking chain of water about 7 miles long.

A fifth reservoir, Claerwen, was completed in 1952. You have to take a detour up a tributary valley to see this 4-mile-long lake, set in bleak moorland west of Caban-coch. Claerwen's dam – which measures 355m (1166ft) in length by 56m (184ft) in height – is a colossal structure, which has doubled the storage capacity of these lakes from 50,000 million litres (11,000 million gallons) to 100,000 million litres (22,000 million gallons) of water.

Elan Valley Visitor Centre, Elan village. Tel (0597) 810880/810898. F. Excellent centre with first-class facilities. Interesting exhibitions on water, wildlife and history, audio-visual theatre, picnic sites, walks, tourist information.

Learn all about the lakes and their surrounding countryside at the Elan Valley Visitor Centre

ERWOOD

POWYS   E5

This pretty village, on the banks of the river Wye in prime fishing country, has surprising literary associations. It is said that the idea for the magazine *Punch* was conceived here when Henry Mayhew, its proprietor, was staying at a local inn. Minor roads to the west lead into the bare Mynydd Epynt mountain range; eastwards, there is a gentler landscape of rolling border country.

FAIRBOURNE

GWYNEDD   C2

This small seaside resort commands superb views of mountains, sea and estuary. It is known to all railway enthusiasts as the home of the Fairbourne and Barmouth Steam Railway, which has the narrowest of narrow gauges – only 31.11cm (12¼in). It was built in 1890 by the flour manufacturer Sir Arthur McDougall as a horse-drawn tramway to carry building materials to Porth Penrhyn at the mouth of the Mawddach estuary. Steam power was introduced in 1916.

Fairbourne's superbly-crafted locomotives – mainly steam – are half-size replicas of famous narrow-gauge railway engines. They run for 2 miles across the dunes to Porth Penrhyn, connecting with a ferry for Barmouth, making this the last narrow-gauge boat train in Europe! The train stops off en route at a halt with the world's longest station name, verified by no less a source than the *Guinness Book of Records*: Gorsafawddacha'idraigodanheddogleddollônpenrhynareurdraethceredigion (The Mawddach Station with its dragon's teeth on

Sweeping sands at Fairbourne

the northerly Penrhyn Drive on the golden beach of Cardigan Bay). The 'dragon's teeth' are concrete defences left over from World War II.

Fairbourne has a fine stretch of sands and there are plenty of walks up into the foothills of Cader Idris. St Cynon's Church is more modern than it looks – it was built in 1927 through a bequest, and has handsome stone arches in various shades of grey and brown.

Birdland (at narrow-gauge railway station). Tel (0341) 250362. C. Largest walk-in aviary in Wales with huge variety of birds – waterfowl, peacocks, parrots, exotic species.

Fairbourne and Barmouth Steam Railway. Tel (0341) 250362. C. A treat for all railway buffs, with memorable views along the way. Victorian-style terminus, period observation coach. Engines can be viewed in loco shed.

Ride to the mouth of the Mawddach on the Fairbourne and Barmouth Steam Railway

FURNACE

DYFED   D3

The large barn-like building beside the A487 gives Furnace its unusual name. This is a historic metal-smelting site, dating from the 17th century when silver refining took place here. The present building was put up in the mid-18th century as an iron foundry (the iron ore was probably shipped from Cumbria). Air was pumped into its charcoal-fired blast furnace by bellows powered by a waterwheel. The restored foundry still has a waterwheel, though this dates from a later period when the building was converted into a sawmill.

Dyfi Furnace

In the foundry's dramatic interior you can walk along the charging platform and peer down into the furnace itself. Outside, the old leat leads to picturesque falls on the river Einion.

The beautiful wooded valley through which the Einion flows is known as Cwm Einion or Artists' Valley (it was popular with painters 100 years ago). A narrow dead-end road climbs up past the foundry, following the river into the forested foothills of the Plynlimon mountain range.

Near the furnace, on the opposite side of the road, is the entrance to the Royal Society for the Protection of Birds' Ynyshir Nature Reserve. Its 364 hectares (900 acres) of varied habitats – saltmarsh, oak woodland and open hillsides – attract breeding birds, wintering birds of prey and spring and autumn migrants.

Dyfi Furnace. C. Charcoal-fired blast furnace, used for smelting iron between c.1755 and the early 1800s. ✥

GANLLWYD

GWYNEDD   D2

You should bring your walking boots to Ganllwyd, a pretty village on the A470 surrounded by the trees of the Coed y Brenin Forest. Although now a Forestry Commission plantation, Coed y Brenin is not the usual dense mass of regimented conifers. In medieval times, the forest was an estate of the Welsh princes. Rivers rush through its hills and hidden valleys, which contain copses of ancient

oakwoods and other deciduous trees as well as the ubiquitous evergreen. This is hilly country, with constantly changing landscapes, viewpoints, and a marvellous network of forest walks.

A bridge across the river Mawddach just south of the village leads to the Ty'n-y-groes picnic site, the starting point of a number of walks. There is a similar starting point at Pont Dolgefeiliau beside the river Eden a mile or so north of Ganllwyd. Coed y Brenin has long associations with Welsh gold. Set off from Pont Dolgefeiliau for the beauty spot, deep in the heart of the forest, where abandoned workings from the 19th-century heyday of gold mining stand close to two lovely waterfalls, Pistyll Cain and Rhaeadr Mawddach.

Coed y Brenin possibly has the best visitor facilities of any forest in Wales. All in all, there are over 50 miles of waymarked walks, not to mention an arboretum, nature reserve and forest visitor centre. The latter should be your first port of call for detailed information on this attractive 35-square-mile woodland.

From Ganllwyd, it is only a short walk of ¼ mile to Rhaeadr Ddu (The Black Waterfall) – aptly named, for the river Gamlan tumbles over black rocks in a valley of tall oaks.

Nearby
Coed y Brenin Visitor Centre (off A470 2 miles north of Ganllwyd). Tel (0341) 40666. F. Forest displays featuring wildlife, geology and gold mining. Audio-visual show, picnic sites, trails.

Waymarked paths in Coed y Brenin lead to waterfalls hidden in the heart of the forest

GWBERT

DYFED   A5/B5

Gwbert is a beautifully sited hamlet overlooking the
Teifi estuary near Cardigan, with hotel and guest
house accommodation. There are bracing walks
along the grassy cliffs and views across the estuary
to Poppit Sands and Cemaes Head at the start of the
Pembrokeshire Coast National Park.

In the days when schooners and brigs sailed the
seven seas from Cardigan, this estuary was crowded
with vessels. A trim blue-and-white coastguard
station reminds us that vigilance is still needed along
this cliff-backed shoreline. Cardigan Island, off the
northern headland, is a wildlife refuge noted for its
seals, sea-birds and unusual breed of Soay sheep.

HARLECH i

GWYNEDD   C1

Harlech is a distinctive and attractive town whose
fame is out of all proportion to its size. It has a well-
known golf club, the Royal St David's; but its
celebrity derives mainly – and understandably – from
its magnificent castle dramatically set on a high
crag, with Snowdon and her sister peaks as a
backdrop. This was one of the strongholds built by
Edward I after his conquest of Wales late in the 13th
century. Today it ranks as a World Heritage Listed
Site, a place of universal value.

Amazingly, the castle – painted a dazzling white
when new – was raised in only seven years. The first
stone was laid in May 1283, six months after the
death of Llywelyn, the prince who had united Wales
in a struggle against English rule. It was the creation
of an architectural genius, Master James of St
George, the outstanding castle builder of his time.
He made cunning use of the site's natural defences,
blending these with man-made fortifications
embodying the most up-to-date principles of
military architecture. It should have been impregna-
ble, yet 120 years later it was captured by Owain
Glyndŵr, the warrior prince who briefly gave Wales
a parliament and forged an alliance with France.

The castle was recaptured and the Glyndŵr
rebellion was crushed, but Harlech came back into
prominence in the Wars of the Roses, being held by
the Lancastrians until its surrender in 1468 after a
long siege by the Yorkists. Tradition says it was this
struggle that inspired the song *Men of Harlech*.

The Civil War between King and Parliament
nearly two centuries later saw the castle being
defended by the Royalist Colonel William Owen,
until a besieging force led by Colonel Mytton forced
its surrender in 1647. Fortunately an order for its
demolition was not carried out, and the castle today
is remarkably well preserved.

Harlech is in the Snowdonia National Park, and
there are marvellous views from the castle battle-
ments and wall walks across Tremadog Bay to the
spine of the Llŷn peninsula and landwards to

Harlech Castle, still a formidable sight after all these years

Snowdon itself. As you stand facing west the Royal St David's links are below you, with the rolling dunes beyond. Remember that when the castle was built, the sea was much nearer than it is today. Just how close it came isn't precisely known, but the existence of the Water Gate at the foot of the castle rock near the railway station is proof of direct access for shipping, possibly along a channel.

The sculpture near the castle entrance, *The Two Kings*, by Ivor Roberts, is based on a story in the 'Mabinogion', the classical collection of Welsh folk tales from the distant past. History apart, one of the glories of Harlech is its fine stretch of sands, ideal for beach games. Two miles south at Llandanwg is the tiny 'church in the dunes', St Tanwg's, with services only a few times a year.

Harlech Castle. Tel (0766) 780552. C. Concentric castle with wall walk providing unforgettable views of sea and mountains. Highly atmospheric, with rooks and jackdaws flapping around the towers. Artillery platforms for stone-throwing machines on western edge of rock. Exhibition interpreting castle's history. ✚

Harlech Swimming Pool and Sports Centre. Tel (0766) 780576. C. Indoor pool, sauna/solarium and sports facilities.

Theatr Ardudwy, Coleg Harlech. Tel (0766) 780667. Theatre with wide-ranging entertainments programme, including films, music and plays.

Nearby
Muriau'r Gwyddelod (Irishmen's Walls). F. Prehistoric hut circles in hills 1¹/₂ miles south of Harlech. Difficult to locate without Ordnance Survey map.

Old Llanfair Quarry Slate Caverns. Tel (0766) 780247. C. Self-guided tours of awesome series of slate caverns, some with majestic names like 'The Cathedral'. Spooky in places but memorable. Hard hat and torch provided.

KERRY
POWYS   F3

At first sight, Kerry is an unremarkable place: a quiet community strung alongside the road from Newtown into England and surrounded by the hills of Mid Wales. But the name of Kerry is highly respected in the woollen industry for its breed of black-muzzled sheep which has won prize after prize in agricultural shows. Kerry Hill sheep have very white wool, suitable for light dyes and used to make fine Welsh flannels.

On the edge of the village is the old 19th-century Reading Room, now converted into houses. The neo-Gothic façade has three impressive lancet windows, and a stone inscription set in the wall pays tribute to John Naylor of Leighton Hall and Brynllywarch. He was the benefactor who paid for the building, which when first erected in 1868 was part of the village school. The main school building, across the road, still serves its original purpose and has a modern extension designed to complement its Victorian style.

KNIGHTON
POWYS   F4

Knighton is Welsh, but only just: it sits on the modern Wales-England border, as well as on the more ancient boundary of Offa's Dyke. The town's Welsh name, Tref-y-Clawdd, means 'Town of the Dyke', and this is a good starting point for walks along the 8th-century barrier put up by King Offa of Mercia as a dividing line between his kingdom and Welsh territory.

Offa's earthen wall and ditch ran for much of the length of Wales from Chepstow to Prestatyn (the present border, incidentally, only coincides roughly with the line of the dyke). As well as being a political barrier, the dyke served as a kind of customs point, controlling the movement of cattle and trade.

Remnants of this ancient earthwork can still be seen in many locations along the border. One of its best-preserved sections is at Llanfair Hill, about 5 miles north of Knighton, where the top of the bank to the bottom of the ditch measures 5m (16ft). The Offa's Dyke Heritage Centre, housed in an old primary school on West Street, gives information on short walks and has a small exhibition on the dyke's history. In the Riverside Park behind the centre a stone monument marks the opening of the 168-mile Offa's Dyke Long-Distance Path in 1971.

Knighton is the only original settlement on Offa's Dyke, and today there is still a distinctly medieval look to the town, which clings to the side of a steep hill above the river Teme. St Edward's Church sits at the bottom of the hill, and the main road climbs past a 19th-century clock tower set in the middle of the bustling marketplace. From here it's a long haul up the traffic-free Tudor 'Narrows', now lined with small shops, to the summit, where a Norman castle once stood.

At Bryn-y-Castell (Castle Hill), next to the town's community centre, there are more extensive remains

The Welsh hills begin at Knighton

of a second castle, also dating from the Norman Conquest. Look out for the Old House on High Street, a traditional narrow, half-timbered building squeezed between an antiques gallery and a butcher's shop.

Regular attractions in Knighton include the May Fair and annual Agricultural Show and Carnival, when the town crier takes to the streets in full voice and finery.

Offa's Dyke Heritage Centre, West Street. Tel (0547) 528192. F. Exhibition, library and audio-visual room showing films and slide shows.

LAKE VYRNWY
POWYS   E2

This spectacular man-made lake, known in Welsh as Llyn Efyrnwy, is a vast expanse of water, fringed with thick woodland, filling the top of the remote, mountain-locked Vyrnwy valley. Before Liverpool Corporation built the reservoir to meet its city's urgent need for water, this was the setting for Llanwddyn, a quiet community of about 440 people. In 1877 George Deacon, Liverpool's Borough and Water Engineer, advised the council that flooding this fertile spot would provide the cheapest solution to its problems. The original village was levelled – though traces can still be seen when the reservoir waters are very low – and new houses were built

lower down the valley. Even the bodies from the old cemetery were reburied, as the valley floor was cleared for construction of the dam, which took eight years and claimed 44 lives.

The massive walls of the dam now carry traffic from one side of the valley to the other, and in the distance the neo-Gothic water tower looms over the lake's inky water like a Bavarian fortress. Up to 205 million litres (45 million gallons) flow from the lake to Liverpool every day.

Llanwddyn Chapel, which was re-erected by a Liverpool architect in 1888, now houses the Vyrnwy Visitor Centre, where the full story of the village and reservoir is told in an exhibition and small audio-visual display. A map sketched from memory by the village schoolmaster shows the layout of the original Llanwddyn, which occupied an area inhabited by man for about 4000 years.

The Vyrnwy valley is a prime attraction for birdwatchers: a Royal Society for the Protection of Birds hide has been set up opposite the visitor centre, and the Craig Garth-bwlch and Grwn-Oer nature trails explore the surrounding hills and woodlands. The wild country above the lake is part of the most extensive stretch of heather moorland still in existence in Wales.

Vyrnwy Visitor Centre (off B4393). Tel (069173) 278. F. Exhibition on history and workings of reservoir, past village life and wildlife in the valley, including audio-visual display.

Lake Vyrnwy, with its fairytale water tower

Forestry work explained at the Coed y Brenin Visitor Centre

Bwlch Nant-yr-Arian stands above the beautiful Vale of Rheidol

Take a walk through the woods

Coed y Brenin, Dyfi, Dyfnant, Hafren, Rheidol, Ystwyth . . . these are the names of some of the conifer forests of Mid Wales. There are those who criticize the number of commercial forest plantations in Wales, though it must be said that the Forestry Commission is aware of the environmental impact of its work, and has made major efforts to open up its woodlands for leisure and recreational purposes.

Car parks and attractive picnic sites have been established amongst the trees. Many of these sites are starting points for waymarked forest walks, which can range from short strolls suitable for all the family to long hikes for enthusiastic walkers. At Coed y Brenin north of Dolgellau, for example, there's a network of over 50 miles of waymarked trails.

Conifers aren't the only thing you'll see on these forest walks. The Coed y Brenin trails lead to waterfalls and old gold mines. There are scenic riverside paths and a spectacular ridge walk in the Rheidol Forest, while the Hafren Forest reveals the source of the mighty river Severn to those prepared to trudge across rough ground. Woodland wildlife is explained on many short walks – some only a mile or so in length – which have been specially established to encourage the public to venture into the forests.

Other attractive features to look out for include a forest nature reserve at Coed y Brenin, where a 300-hectare (741-acre) stretch of diverse forest habitat with a wildlife observation hide has been established.

Coed y Brenin has particularly good visitor facilities. Call in first at the Coed y Brenin Visitor Centre, located just off the A470 near Ganllwyd, 8 miles north of Dolgellau. Attractive displays provide an introduction to the life, work and wildlife of the forest.

The Bwlch Nant-yr-Arian Visitor Centre off the A44 near Ponterwyd 10 miles from Aberystwyth fulfils a similar role for the Rheidol Forest. This spectacularly sited centre – it's worth visiting for the view alone – tells the story of the forest by tape/slide presentations, dioramas and pictures. The centre is also the starting point for a number of attractive woodland walks.

33

LAMPETER

DYFED   **C5**

Lampeter is a country town where students brush shoulders with farmers, as it is the home of St David's University College. Founded in 1822, it is the oldest and smallest of the colleges that together make up the University of Wales. The town combines simplicity with a certain amount of sophistication, and the local businesses reflect this. There are homely cafés and more upmarket bistros, old coaching inns and shops to suit a variety of tastes. Locally made crafts include woven materials and furniture.

The substantial town houses of Bridge Street, the main route in from the south, reflect the solid respectability of Victorian Lampeter. High Street has the Black Lion and the Royal Oak, both with archways under which stagecoaches used to clatter into cobbled yards. Harford Square, at the intersection of these streets, is named after one of the families of local gentry who in bygone days ran local affairs in patrician style.

Lampeter stands on the river Teifi, which was the dividing line between the old counties of Cardiganshire and Carmarthenshire.

Nearby
*Cae Hir Gardens, Cribyn. Tel (0570) 470839. C.
2¹/₂ hectares (6 acres) of attractive hillside gardens,
ingeniously landscaped with stone walls and
benches. Take A475 Newcastle Emlyn road, then
B4337 at Llanwnnen.*

LLANARMON DYFFRYN CEIRIOG

CLWYD   **F1**

One of Wales's best-loved poets was born here in 1832. John Hughes, known by his bardic name Ceiriog, wrote sentimental verses to some of the most poignant old Welsh melodies, including 'Dafydd y Garreg Wen' (David of the White Rock). His birthplace is a beautiful and isolated village in the Ceiriog valley, and his life is commemorated on a plaque in the unusual church, which has an austere design but two pulpits.

Llyn Cwm Bychan, in the mountains above Llanbedr

A 1000-year-old yew tree grows in the churchyard, which is laid out alongside the Ceiriog river. The village itself is well cared for, with flowers decorating the streets and houses.

LLANBEDR

GWYNEDD   **C1**

Llanbedr is an attractive village of mellow stone 3 miles south of Harlech, with sea on one side and mountains on the other. South of the bridge in the centre of the village is Mochras – better known as Shell Island for the amazing variety of sea shells on its beaches. It's an island only at high water, as it can be reached by way of a causeway the rest of the time.

If you prefer the mountains, turn off the main road by the Victoria Inn in Llanbedr. This takes you up the lovely Artro valley to Llyn Cwm Bychan, a small lake in the rugged mountains behind Harlech. East of the lake you'll find hundreds of steps cut into the mountainside. These are the Roman Steps, part of an ancient trackway between Harlech and Bala. Modern scholarship has dealt a blow to local legend: it's now believed that these were laid not by the Romans but in medieval times, as a pack-horse route.

Llanbedr's long links with the RAF can be seen from the road to Shell Island, which skirts an air base.

*Maes Artro Village. Tel (034123) 467. C. Spacious
complex in a time warp, with eggs – not for sale! –
at a shilling (5p) a dozen in the Village of Yester-
year, and a prominently sited Spitfire. Originally an
RAF World War II base – RAF Museum has sounds
and sights of the war. Old farm implements
exhibition, complete with spiked mole trap.
Aquarium. Totem poles in adventure playground.
Outdoor draughts with giant timber pieces. Craft
shops.*

Nearby
*Shell Island (Mochras). Tel (034123) 217. C. Has the
feel of a real island, with springy grass and sea-
birds galore. Plenty of wild flowers as well as shells.
Good fishing, bathing. 'Island' is cut off at high tide
– look out for safe crossing times at beginning of
causeway.*

LLANBISTER

POWYS   E4

Llanbister spreads down a hill towards the river Ithon from its church, St Cynllo's, which has a chimney instead of the usual tower at its western end. The tower sits at the east of the mainly 13th-century building, which originally served as a fortress as well as a place of worship, in the days when skirmishes between English and Welsh focused on this troubled Marcher region. A wide flight of stone steps leads to the sombre church interior, where you can see the remnants of a bassoon and double bass once used to accompany hymns from the minstrels' gallery, which still exists.

Below the village, about a mile towards Newtown on the A483, is an unexpected treat. The little church at Llananno, huddled down beside the main road, has an elaborate carved rood screen more fitted to a large cathedral. Dating from the 15th or 16th century, the screen was taken down in 1877 while Llananno was rebuilt, and it is possible to make out new sections of oak at each end, added to fill the width of the church. The new work includes a row of Biblical figures inserted into the screen's original niches. At the western end of the church there is a holy water stoup built into the wall, and a churchwarden's box pew, now the vestry, inscribed for David Lewis, warden in 1681.

Llananno Church's magnificent rood screen

LLANDDEWI BREFI

DYFED   D4

The imposing Church of St David seems to overwhelm this sleepy little village. It stands on a prominent rise above the village square in a spot that has famous religious associations. St David, Wales's patron saint, held a meeting here in AD519 to denounce the Pelagian heresy. During this Synod of Brefi, he had difficulty in addressing the crowd, so the ground is said to have risen beneath his feet in order that he could be better seen and heard; a case, perhaps, of the location helping to explain the legend.

The church was built around a late 12th-century tower with later additions. A statue of Dewi Sant (St David), staff in hand and with a dove on his shoulder, stands in a corner near the main door. The church also contains an impressive collection of early

Llanddewi Brefi, transformed into a Welsh marketplace during the filming of the TV series We Are Seven

Celtic Christian stones (7th–10th century) inscribed with ancient Ogham markings.

LLANDINAM

POWYS   E3

It's easy to see why Llandinam has been awarded, on more than one occasion, the title of 'Best Kept Village in Wales'. Neat and colourful gardens line the A470 alongside the river Severn, and surround the black-and-white timbered houses of the village centre, set well back from the main road. Llandinam's residents take a lively interest in the area's history and associations, and a temporary exhibition is held each summer in the brick-and-timber village hall. Beside the old railway station, a statue of David Davies (1818–90) testifies to the remarkable success of this locally born entrepreneur, who made his fortune from coal and was responsible for building the Barry docks in South Wales. The statue is the work of Sir Alfred Gilbert, who was also responsible for *Eros* in London's Piccadilly Circus.

Llandinam's higgledy-piggledy little street and immaculate flower displays are overlooked by St Llonio's Church, where a scheme to tidy up the graveyard recently won the villagers a Prince of Wales Award. The churchyard was divided into 24 sections, each one maintained by a family or individual. On the upper bank – said to be part of a pre-Roman defence – a memorial marks the resting place of Davies's granddaughters, Margaret and Gwendoline, well-known philanthropists who founded the Gregynog Chair of Music at the University College of Aberystwyth and gave their home to the University of Wales (see Tregynon entry).

LLANDRILLO

CLWYD   E1

Llandrillo stands in the undisturbed Vale of Edeyrnion between Bala and Corwen. The fertile farmlands of the vale contrast with the exposed, open moorlands of the Berwyn Mountains rising to the east. Walkers can set off from the village for the heights of Cadair Bronwen and Cadair Berwyn, about 3¹/₂ miles to the south-east.

35

Fans of Victorian architecture can hardly believe their eyes when they are first introduced to Llandrindod Wells. This is *the* perfectly preserved Victorian town from top to bottom. It's a showcase for all the classic features – the tall gables, the decorative ironwork, the glass canopies, the red and yellow bricks, the ornamental gardens, and the wide streets purpose built for promenading. The description 'purpose built' is the key to Llandrindod's personality. Llandrindod – shortened to Llandod by the locals – was created from almost nothing in mid-Victorian times as a purpose-built spa town.

The town, a bastion of Victorian Britain, seems at odds with its surroundings on the doorstep of Welsh hill sheep farming country. Llandrindod prospered as 'taking the waters' became fashionable and rail travel opened up parts of Wales to a new tourist market. It soon grew into the premier of a quartet of Mid Wales spa towns (the other 'Wells' towns are Builth, Llanwrtyd and Llangammarch). According to an old advertisement, Llandrindod's 'splendid, bracing air and the saline, sulphur, magnesian and chalybeate waters are very efficacious in the treatment of gout, rheumatism, anaemia, neurasthenia, dyspepsia, diabetes and liver affections'.

'Taking the waters', though, was often only a pretence for having a good time. Llandrindod was a popular inland resort with a host of attractive amenities that can still be enjoyed today. The Rock Park Gardens, for example, are only a short walk from the main streets. These lovely gardens, in a wooded dell, lead to a viewpoint known as Lover's Leap, a spectacular cliff above a huge bend in the river Ithon.

But you can't get away from the waters. A chalybeate spring issues from the mouth of a lion in a drinking fountain in the gardens. A greater variety of waters is on offer at the Rock Park Spa, whose pump house tea rooms have been restored to their former glory. Three waters are on draught – saline, sulphur and magnesium – served from a marble counter.

Other legacies from Llandrindod's heyday as an inland resort include a large boating and fishing lake, spacious parks and excellent facilities for tennis, bowls and golf. These have recently been added to by a large indoor bowls centre. Llandrindod's museum, in the old library, recalls the town's thriving past and also contains finds from the Roman camp of Castell Collen, a mile away.

The inhabitants of Llandrindod guard their Victorian heritage closely, and are seizing every opportunity to preserve it. An old Victorian signal box, which stood on the edge of town, has been

Llandrindod relives its past during its annual Victorian Festival

The lake, Llandrindod

relocated at the railway station. The Victorian theme is also carried into the Tourist Information Centre, where displays and a video presentation provide an introduction to the spa town. Each year the town relives its past during a week-long Victorian festival, held in August. Another legacy from the old days is plentiful accommodation. Llandrindod now serves as a well-located touring centre for the Mid Wales mountains, Elan valley lakes and the nearby Brecon Beacons.

Lear's Magic Lantern Theatre. Tel (0597) 824737. C. Victorian-style entertainment – projection theatre, museum and tea room.

Llandrindod Wells Museum. Tel (0597) 824513. F. Memorabilia from the town's spa days.

Rock Park Spa. Tel (0597) 824729. C. Your chance to 'take the waters' in authentic period setting.

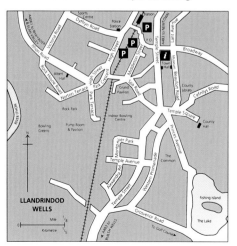

LLANDYSUL
DYFED   C5

Llandysul has the air of a town still rooted in its old country ways. Its long main shopping street has a quiet dignity and pleasing variety, scarcely any two buildings being alike. Note the squat, no-nonsense look of Ebenezer Chapel, built in 1833. The offices of the Gomer Press, long-established Welsh publishers, are on the opposite side of the street.

Running parallel, at a lower level, is the road providing access to St Tysul's Church. This is well worth a visit for the beauty of its interior. Built in Early English style, it has massive square pillars with pointed arches. There are some flowery inscriptions to the local gentry of bygone days and an ancient altar stone with incised markings in the Lady Chapel.

The church has had secular as well as religious uses. Two centuries ago the porch served as one of the goals for a no-holds-barred annual football match. The old Welsh game of 'chware pel' was played around the church tower and a sexton of the early 18th century claimed to be able to throw the ball right over the top.

Llandysul is in an area that once abounded with woollen mills, some of which remain to keep the tradition alive.

Nearby
Castell Howell Family Club, Pont-siân (off B4459). Tel (054555) 209. C. Swimming pool, squash, horse riding and other facilities in a complex centred on converted farm buildings.

Maesllyn Woollen Mill Museum, Maesllyn (off A486 Llandysul–Ffostrasol road). Tel (023975) 251. C. 19th-century mill built in Yorkshire style by local magnate. Revived in 1976 after closure. Demonstrations of hand weaving and displays of old machinery. Collections of radio sets and sewing machines are added attractions. Craft shop, picnic and play areas.

Y Felin Wlan (Rock Mills), Capel Dewi (off B4459). Tel (0559) 362356. F. Family-run firm founded a century ago, with working waterwheel driven by river Clettwr. Products on sale in the craft shop. Appealing down-to-earth atmosphere.

LLANEGRYN
GWYNEDD   C2

An amazing example of medieval craftsmanship is to be found in this village in the shape of the local church's intricately carved oak rood screen, a work of awesome complexity. It divides the nave from the chancel and is one of the few surviving rood screens in Wales, most having been destroyed either at the time of the Reformation or by Victorian restorers. There is no documentary evidence to support the claim that it came from Cymer Abbey near Dolgellau.

The church is beautifully sited on a hill just outside the village. Turn off the A493 into Llanegryn, then go left immediately after crossing the stone bridge. Drive up the narrow lane and take the second turning on the left.

LLANFAIR CAEREINION
POWYS   E2

Llanfair Caereinion grew up as a flannel-producing centre in the 18th and 19th centuries. The pleasant little riverside town, located in the Banwy valley, is an unhurried place surrounded by hilly border country. It is the main terminus for the Welshpool and Llanfair Light Railway, a narrow-gauge line that runs for 8 miles to Welshpool. The railway was opened in 1903 to carry local people and their produce to market, and, like many of Wales's 'Great Little Trains', was saved from extinction by a group of dedicated enthusiasts. There is an attractive riverside walk from the station.

North-east of the town, the Banwy joins the river Vyrnwy at the entrance to a beautiful, broad valley, lined with wooded hills, known as the Vale of Meifod.

Welshpool and Llanfair Light Railway. Tel (0938) 810441. C. Follows a steeply graded route over the hills to the Severn valley.

Ride on a narrow-gauge line to Welshpool

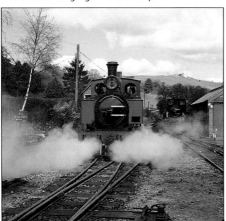

Llanfyllin Bird and Butterfly World

from Narrow Street, where there are two fine old buildings: an early Georgian manor house and, nearby, The Hall, built on the site of the Elizabethan Plas Ucha' (Upper Court). Details of several self-guided walks in the town and local nature trails are available from the Tourist Information Centre.

Llanfyllin's parish church is a simple 18th-century building in mellow brick, and the Pendref Congregational Chapel was originally established in 1640. It was here that Ann Griffiths, the prolific hymn writer, was converted in 1796. From her farmstead home at Dolanog, between Llanfyllin and Llanwddyn, she wrote 70 hymns, still popular and remarkable for their elegance and passion, before she died at the early age of 29.

Nearby
Llanfyllin Bird and Butterfly World, Domgay. Tel (069184) 751. C. Birds and butterflies from all the world. 50 aviaries. Play area for children. No dogs allowed.

LLANGAMMARCH WELLS
POWYS   E5

Llangammarch was the smallest of Mid Wales's spa centres. Unlike its bigger brother Llandrindod, there are few clues in sleepy Llangammarch to remind us of its flourishing past.

Llangammarch developed as a spa for two reasons – its mineral springs and the railway. You can still reach the village by rail, for it is located on the Heart of Wales line, one of British Rail's most scenic routes, which links Swansea with Shrewsbury. This railway carried Llangammarch's 19th-century visitors, who came here for waters that contained barium chloride, a rare element that supposedly helped in the cure of heart disease, rheumatism and gout.

Today's visitors come for the fishing (the Irfon is a good trout river) and the tranquillity of the surroundings. Llangammarch stands at the northern end of Mynydd Epynt, a large, empty area of high moorland used as a training ground by the army. A public road across this brooding moorland climbs up a steep-sided valley from Llangammarch. From the summit, there are glorious views looking northwards and eastwards across Mid Wales's mountains and borderlands.

LLANFYLLIN
POWYS   E2

Visitors are well catered for in the exceptionally pretty town of Llanfyllin. Cheerfully painted hotels and shops line the main street, and in summer a show of flowers decorates gardens, windowsills and doorways at every turn, against the dramatic backdrop of the Berwyn foothills.

Although it is a community of only about 1200, Llanfyllin has been a town since 1293, and elects its own mayor. This privilege is due to the fact that its charter was granted by a native Welsh ruler, the Lord of Mechain. Seven centuries earlier, Llanfyllin's original church and a holy well were established by St Myllin, the first person in Britain to baptize by immersion. The restored well, overlooking the beautiful Cain valley, can be reached along a lane

MYTHS AND LEGENDS

The silence of the Mid Wales hills is deceptive. If this landscape could talk, it would tell tales of devilish deeds and drowned kingdoms. Devil's Bridge takes its name from a story in which a crafty old woman outwitted Satan. Aberdovey is associated with the legend of a kingdom, lost beneath the waves when the keeper of its sea wall ignored his duties during a great storm 1500 years ago. Sometimes, distant chimes can be heard from the sea – the Bells of Aberdovey.

Mid Wales's moody vistas have inspired many folk tales and legends

Wales's earliest written folk tales appear in the 'Mabinogion', stories told around the fireside before they were recorded on manuscript in medieval times. One cautionary tale recalls the disasters caused by an ill-matched marriage between Welsh and Irish nobility, a story that began promisingly enough when 13 'beautiful, seemly' ships sailed from Ireland to Harlech.

Dramatic landscapes have always been a powerful stimulus to the storyteller. The brooding, rock-strewn heights of Cader Idris (The Chair of Idris) above Dolgellau were the domain of Idris, the giant skilled in poetry,

philosophy and astronomy. Walkers should be aware that anyone who dares spend a night on his summit will end up as a poet, madman or corpse. Cader Idris also has a Welsh version of the Loch Ness story. The lake of Llyn Cau, below the summit, reputedly contains a monster that seized a poor swimmer in the 18th century.

Some legends are based on physical features, other tales have a firm foundation in fact. The prominent mound on which Llanddewi Brefi's church is built is in the former category. This mound was supposedly caused in the 6th century when the ground rose beneath St David's feet so that he could address the crowds. On the other hand, we know for certain that the 'Red Robbers of Mallwyd' really existed (the Brigands' Inn in the village is named after them). These red-haired brigands terrorized the area in the 16th century before many of them were executed, thanks to the efforts of Baron Lewis Owen. The baron was subsequently murdered by surviving members of the gang at Llidiart-y-Barwn (The Baron's Gate) $2^1/_2$ miles to the east (near the hairpin bend along the A458).

Aberdovey's sands lead down to a 'lost kingdom' beneath the waves

LLANGRANNOG

DYFED   **B4**

Cardigan Bay at its most spectacular at Llangrannog

Llangrannog stands as close to the sea as possible, as if ready to take a plunge. It is a beguiling village where neat whitewashed houses and inns overlook a small sandy beach between fern-clad cliffs. The away-from-it-all feeling is so strong that it is hard to imagine this as a hive of industry, yet in the last century the narrow streets rang with the hammer and clatter of shipbuilders, and the Pentre Arms has a list of the schooners and other ocean-going craft registered at Llangrannog.

A choice of winding country roads leading off the A487 Cardigan–Aberystwyth route takes you down to the village, which is built on two levels. The upper part, about 275m (300 yards) above the beach, has a church with a bellcote and a handsome Calvinist chapel of 1863. The village Post Office overlooks a stream where a fence has been imaginatively created out of cast iron wheels from old farm implements. The village is the home of a holiday centre run by Urdd Gobaith Cymru (The Welsh League of Youth).

One of the delights of Llangrannog is the wonderful cliff walk to Ynys Lochtyn, a secluded promontory owned by the National Trust.

Llangrannog Ski Centre. Tel (0239) 654473. C. Dry ski slope at holiday centre belonging to the Urdd (Welsh League of Youth). Beautifully sited overlooking Cardigan Bay. Look out for signpost just above village.

LLANGURIG

POWYS   **E3**

Two major roads cross at Llangurig: the north–south (A470) and the east–west (A44) routes across Wales. An old railway bridge recalls a less successful link across country: this village was to have been on the line to Aberystwyth, where there were ambitious plans to capture the 19th-century tourist trade. The scheme went awry when the task of building a railway track across Mid Wales's forbiddingly wild terrain proved too costly.

Llangurig's church, founded in the 6th century, was under the rule of monks from Strata Florida Abbey from 1180. Today's building is a 19th-century restoration, but the huge square bell-tower dates from the 14th century, and its three bells were cast in 1700. A 13th-century lancet forms part of the window to the west of the south door.

The village is the first settlement of any real size on the river Wye, whose source is in the hills to the north-west. Eisteddfa-gurig, 8 miles west along the A44, is the starting point for the ascent of Plynlimon, a remote, misty summit 752m (2468ft) high.

LLANGYNOG

POWYS   **E1**

Llangynog is a peaceful hill-farming community, sheltered by the dramatic Berwyn mountain peaks, which serves as a watering-hole for travellers on their way to Bala. There are a couple of cafés here, and two interesting inns: the 1751 New Inn and its older neighbour, the Tanat Valley Inn, dating from the 16th century.

Two miles to the north-west on a minor road, well signposted from Llangynog, is the intriguing church of Pennant Melangell in its circular church-yard. The church, hemmed in by wooded hills, is currently being restored, but the medieval effigy of St Melangell can still be seen. Look closely and you will see two hares peeping from under the carved robes: Melangell is the patron saint of hares, having saved one of the creatures from a royal huntsman, Prince Brochwel Ysgythrog. The prince was so moved by her action that he presented her with the sacred land where the church now stands. Melangell is said to have been the daughter of an Irish king; the story goes that she fled to Wales to escape marriage and preserve her vows of chastity. Restoration of the Norman church, which houses her shrine, recently uncovered a Romanesque archway linking the chancel and apse.

POWYS   **E3**

Llanidloes's centuries-old market hall, a museum piece on stilts in the middle of town

The first thing that catches your eye in Llanidloes is a black-and-white half-timbered building, sitting on top of hefty timber piers with an open space beneath. This is the town's famous late-16th-century market hall, the only one of its kind surviving in Wales. Markets were held in the covered cobbled area beneath the hall; the old hall itself, in the upper story, has been converted into an endlessly fascinating local museum with a broad – not to say bizarre – range of exhibits. See if you can spot the lamb with two heads!

Amongst other things, the museum tells the story of Llanidloes's mining past. In the 17th century, silver was mined locally. The boom years came after the 1830s, when large increases in the price of lead resulted in a surge in mining activity, and Llanidloes's Van Mines became, for a time, the richest in Britain. Nineteenth-century Llanidloes must have been a busy place, for the town also had a thriving flannel industry. A stone in the old marketplace beneath the museum commemorates visits by John Wesley, who preached from this spot in 1748, 1749 and 1764.

Llanidloes was a hotbed of industrial unrest and an active centre for Chartism, a 19th-century movement set up to campaign for basic democratic rights. Three policemen were specially imported from London, 'a course which combined the maximum of irritation with the minimum of security', to quote one wise commentator. They were captured by the locals and imprisoned for a time at the Trewythen Arms, though the rising was doomed to failure and its three ringleaders transported.

The town's Church of St Idloes, on a religious site founded by the saint in the 7th century, is of medieval origin with a massive 14th-century stone tower capped by a wooden belfry, a feature characteristic of these parts. The church is noteworthy for its splendid early 13th-century arcade of five stone bays, rescued from Abbey Cwmhir (see entry) in the hills to the south.

Look around you in Llanidloes and you will see a pleasing mixture of architectural styles – everything from Elizabethan to Georgian to Victorian – which do not add up to the expected image of a traditional Welsh town. Geography explains the incongruity. Llanidloes might well be situated almost dead-centre in the middle of Wales; but it also stands in an east-west transition zone, where the gentler, softer hills of the border country rise into the misty, exposed wildernesses of the Cambrian Mountains. Llanidloes is a staging-post between cross-border influences – as epitomized by its 'magpie'-style black-and-white buildings – and the 'wild Wales' of remote, robust, stone-built hill sheep farmsteads.

The contrasts between these two worlds is a sharp one, and can be seen if you follow the B4518 mountain road, which climbs steeply out of Llanidloes to the high country around Llyn Clywedog (see entry).

Llanidloes Museum. F. A treasure-chest of exhibits, covering everything from farming to mining, war memorabilia to household implements. Located in a building which is itself a museum piece.

LLANRHAEADR YM MOCHNANT

CLWYD/POWYS   **E1**

Two counties meet here, marking the division between Mid and North Wales. With its intimate atmosphere and low stone cottages which follow the contours of the valley, Llanrhaeadr is a typically Welsh village with a predominantly Welsh-speaking community. It was here that Bishop William Morgan translated the Bible into Welsh in 1588 – an achievement which made a major contribution to

Pistyll Rhaeadr, the highest falls in Wales, in the hills near Llanrhaeadr ym Mochnant

the survival of the language – while he was vicar of the parish. A plaque on the church wall commemorates his association with the area.

A 4-mile road lined with rowan trees leads to the rhaeadr (waterfall) of the village name. Pistyll Rhaeadr, one of the traditional 'Seven Wonders of Wales', is a breathtaking sight, plunging 73m (240ft) in two stages over a sheer cliff, and passing under a 'fairy bridge' – a natural arch of rock – on its way down. At the foot of the waterfall is the pleasant Tan y Pistyll (Under the Spout) tea room, and a footpath leads into the hills, where you can gaze across the Rhaeadr valley to the peaks of the Berwyn Mountains.

It takes a lively imagination to visualize the castle which once stood among wooded hills near Llangedwyn, on the B4396 east of Llanrhaeadr ym Mochnant. An overgrown mound and low earthworks now form part of the surrounding pastureland, but on this spot Owain Glyndŵr, the 14th-/15th-century Welsh leader, once held court. This was Sycharth, immortalized in Welsh verse and folklore as the romantic focal point for the medieval independence movement.

LLANRHYSTYD

DYFED   C4

Set between mountains and sea, Llanrhystyd is a quiet hamlet near Cardigan Bay, with a few services for passing motorists. Attractive stone cottages are grouped around its parish church, whose steeple is easily spotted from the A487 coast road. In the church porch an inscription notes the terms of a £160 rebuilding grant made in the 19th century in return for the reservation of 315 seats 'for the use of the poorer inhabitants of this parish forever'.

A lane leads from Llanrhystyd's church through fields and a caravan park to one half of a pebble beach which is divided in two by the river Wyre. This is a popular area – the beach is sandy at low tide – and there are good views of the coastline. Beyond the beach, part of which is accessible by car, a marked footpath skirts the cliffs above the bay.

Green hills meet the sea at Llanrhystyd

LLANSANTFFRAID YM MECHAIN

POWYS   F2

This large, busy village set in the wide Vyrnwy valley serves as a useful base for exploring the border and Offa's Dyke, and is also popular as a centre for fishermen. Llansantffraid has a lively, almost urban air; at its centre is a block of agro-industrial buildings, a restaurant and a fine art gallery displaying 19th- and early 20th-century paintings.

Towards the Llanfyllin road the atmosphere becomes more rural with a country inn and interesting half-timbered houses. A steep lane leads away from the main road to the church, which has a striking modern stained-glass window at its western end and an ornate Victorian font cover, presented during the restoration of the building in 1893. Below the church clock tower you can see a small 1669 window frame and a stained-glass window with a dedication inscribed in 1619.

LLANUWCHLLYN

GWYNEDD   D1

Helping hands at the Bala Lake Railway

Llanuwchllyn and Bala sit at either end of the 4-mile-long Llyn Tegid (Bala Lake), linked by the narrow-gauge Bala Lake Railway. Two of Llanuwchllyn's sons did much to ensure the survival of the Welsh language in the late 19th and 20th centuries. Sir Owen Edwards, historian and scholar, promoted the use of Welsh literature in schools and was himself an author of many children's books. His son Sir Ifan ab Owen Edwards founded a lasting Welsh institution: Urdd Gobaith Cymru, the Welsh League of Youth, a movement which uses educational courses, outdoor activities and its own national eisteddfod to encourage the use of Welsh by children and teenagers. A statue of the two men stands at the northern end of Llanuwchllyn, and a strikingly designed gate has been erected outside the church in memory of Sir Owen Edwards.

One of the Urdd's permanent camps, Glanllyn, is based by Bala Lake in a mansion which was once home to the Williams-Wynns, who in the 19th century were the greatest landed family in Wales. This politically and territorially powerful family is recalled in an inscription on Llanuwchllyn's village pump, marking the birth of the heir to the Ruabon seat, Wynnstay, and in a plaque on a whitewashed cottage nearby.

At the Bala Lake Railway terminus, south of the village, you can watch the locomotive being prepared for its journey along a lovely lakeside route to Bala. A single trip along the lake's shore takes 25 minutes and can be broken at any of the four stations on the way for swimming, fishing, picnicking or walking.

Bala Lake Railway. Tel (06784) 666. C. Scenic trips on a narrow-gauge track along the shore of Bala Lake.

LLANWRTHWL

POWYS   E4

St Gwrthwl's pretty church is at the centre of this village overlooking the Wye. A stone stepping-stile is built into the wall right next to the gate on the northern side of the churchyard, and an 1878 bell, whose clapper has been worn almost flat over the years, hangs under its own little roof. On the other side of the church, where views open out over wooded hills, is a large boulder, unremarkable in itself but said to have had religious significance for the ancient Britons. Inside the church, four carved faces stare out of an unusual stone font.

The tree-lined road to Hodrid makes a pleasant walk from the village, with glimpses of the river valley below.

LLANWRTYD WELLS

POWYS   D5

The name of this friendly town – reputedly the smallest in Britain – on the edge of the Epynt and Cambrian mountains gives a clue to its past success. This was the westernmost of a chain of spa towns in Mid Wales which brought Victorian health- and pleasure-seekers flocking in on the new railway lines. In summer, Llanwrtyd was a bustling inland resort packed with families from the industrial South Wales valleys and further afield. Few signs remain of the spa fever, apart from respectable 19th-century terraces lined with tall, gabled houses and names such as Victoria Square; not forgetting the overpowering Ffynnon Drewllyd (Smelly Spring) itself, in a beautiful spot beside the river Irfon, which is said to have the highest sulphur content in Britain, and carries a pungent scent which was already well-known as far back as the 14th century.

Explore Llanwrtyd's surroundings on two wheels

Llanwrtyd has emerged from the hectic spa days a quiet, unassuming town, visited mainly for its rural mountain setting. The scenic route which dips and twists for 14 miles from Abergwesyn to Tregaron is one of Wales's most famous drovers' roads, passing over high moorlands known as the 'Roof' or 'Green Desert' of Wales. It was across this barren country that the drovers, tough Welsh 'cowboys', took their cattle from Tregaron to sell at the English markets.

Outdoor activities are a speciality at Llanwrtyd Wells today – from the established annual events, such as Man versus Horse and Four-Day Walks, to tree-lined river walks, from mountain biking to horse riding and pony trekking (Llanwrtyd claims to have 'invented' pony trekking, now a popular pastime across Europe, in the 1950s).

Alongside the A483 on the outskirts of town towards Builth Wells is an old mill by a stream, which is nowadays a shop selling Welsh tweed clothes and tapestries from the Cambrian Factory next door. Free tours show how the wool is sorted, dyed, carded, spun and woven in the factory, originally founded to employ disabled servicemen from the 1914–18 war. In 1927 the workshop was handed over to the British Legion, and a new extension – now the main factory – was added during World War II.

Cambrian Factory. Tel (05913) 211. F. See Welsh flannels being manufactured, and browse through finished products in the shop next door.

DYFED   **C5**

The time to visit Llanybydder is on the last Thursday of every month, when its celebrated horse sales are held. Buyers from all over the country, and further afield, come to this out-of-the-way spot in deepest Dyfed to attend the horse fair, said to be the largest in Britain.

Nearby
Felin yr Aber, Llanwnnen. Tel (0570) 480956. C. Old watermill, producing stoneground flour, set within a traditional small farm. Nature trail, farm machinery displays, picnic area.

Llanybydder's monthly horse fair is a big event, attracting buyers from far and wide

DYFED   **B5**

This idyllic spot in the Teifi valley is a favourite haunt of salmon fishermen. The river flows beneath an ancient five-arch stone bridge, a good place to take the advice of poet W H Davies and 'stand and stare' as long as you can.

GWYNEDD   **C2**

Modern bungalows contrast with stone-built older houses in this village between Tywyn and Fairbourne. There's a sturdy, compact church dating from 1843 notable for its stained-glass windows and gallery. This is the 'new' St Celynnin's Church, the old one being just under 2 miles away at Llangelynnin. The older church is a gem, with its bare, uneven flagstones, wooden benches – not varnished pews – and air of simple piety. The roof is supported by ancient timbers, the walls are whitewashed and parts of pre-Reformation frescoes still survive. Immediately outside the porch is a flat gravestone inscribed with the initials A W, reputedly the burial place of the first Gipsy in Wales.

The church is idyllically placed on a clifftop overlooking the sea. Park in one of the lay-bys on the roadside – don't try to drive down to the church itself.

DYFED   **D5**

If you wanted to explore the remote mountains and high plateaux around this lake in the 1960s, you would have had to do so by foot or horseback. Nowadays, there's a through route from Llandovery northwards, which links up with the Abergwesyn Pass (see Abergwesyn entry). The new road that was constructed across this wilderness area was built at the same time as Llyn Brianne, a huge reservoir completed in 1973 to supply Swansea with water.

A massive, rock-filled dam – the highest of its type in Britain – holds back the headwaters of the Towy and Camddwr rivers, flooding the folds in the mountains in a series of channels that resemble the fingers of an outstretched hand.

You can park above the dam to admire the view and the engineering achievement. The western shores of Llyn Brianne, a haunt of the rare red kite, can be explored on foot. Motorists heading northwards can follow the 'new' road as it climbs and swoops, roller-coaster fashion, along the eastern shores of the lake.

The thickly wooded conical hill at the southern approach to the dam was the hiding place of Twm Siôn Cati, Wales's 16th-century answer to Robin Hood. Twm hid in a cave on Dinas Hill, an obscure spot which is accessible off a circular footpath starting at a small information centre run by the Royal Society for the Protection of Birds (Dinas Hill is an RSPB reserve). A roadside church at Ystrad-ffin stands close to the information centre. This little church, dedicated to St Paulinus, dates from 1117 and once served as a resting place for weary Cistercian monks who trudged across the mountains to Strata Florida Abbey (see Pontrhydfendigaid entry). Sections of their ancient trackway now lie beneath the waters of Llyn Brianne.

Llyn Brianne's waters flood remote hill country

WHAT TO DO ON A RAINY DAY

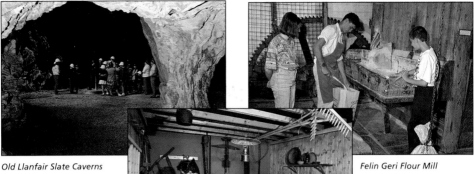

Old Llanfair Slate Caverns

Ceredigion Museum

Felin Geri Flour Mill

It would be pointless to pretend that it doesn't sometimes rain in Mid Wales – the rain, after all, is responsible for all the greenery. But there are plenty of things to keep you occupied – and out of the damp – during the showers. You can, for example, visit a museum-with-a-difference at Aberystwyth – the Ceredigion Museum – which is housed in an old music hall and looks like something out of the 'Good Old Days'.

Powis Castle, at Welshpool, is also full of history. This magnificent National Trust stately home started life in medieval times as a rough-and-ready border castle. Powis's many treasures include exhibits which reflect its associations with Clive of India. Industrial heritage is the theme at the Old Llanfair Quarry Slate Caverns, near Harlech. An impressive system of chambers, caverns and tunnels – which once produced millions of roof slates – can be explored by descending 'Jacob's Ladder'.

A little further down the Cardigan Bay coast is the Maes Artro Village at Llanbedr. There's lots to see and do for all the family at this lively complex, including reminders of its origins as the living quarters of many famous RAF fighter squadrons during World War II.

Aberaeron, at the other end of Cardigan Bay, is the home of a Sea Aquarium and Animal Kingdom Centre, where you'll see local marine life and exotic animals. And if you're interested in bees, then pop into the Honey Bee Exhibition located close by.

Different winged creatures are the objects of attention at Llanfyllin, where the Bird and Butterfly World has a large undercover Tropical House together with many aviaries.

Near Newcastle Emlyn you can call into a water-powered flour mill which produces stoneground flour in the authentic, time-honoured way, or learn all about another traditional rural occupation at the Museum of the Welsh Woollen Industry. And that's not all. In Mid Wales, there are craft workshops to visit, narrow-gauge railways to ride and countryside centres to call into . . . more than enough to keep you entertained whatever the weather.

Powis Castle

45

This 6-mile-long man-made lake, completed in 1967, occupies high, lonely country in the mountains north-west of Llanidloes. Grassy, steep-sided sheep pastures plunge into its waters, which are not only used to supply the Midlands, but also play a recreational role. Trout fishing and sailing are popular at Llyn Clywedog, and there are attractive lakeside trails to follow, one of which goes around the spectacular Ystradhynod headland.

Below the dam – at 72m (237ft) the tallest mass concrete dam in Britain – lie the ruins of the Bryntail Lead Mine, one of many such mines sunk in the Mid Wales hills during the boom years of the last century.

Riding the rapids on the Tryweryn's exciting 'white water' course near Llyn Celyn

Llyn Celyn, in the mountains above Bala, is a 'new' lake created in relatively recent times to supply water to North-east Wales and Cheshire. It doesn't look like a newcomer: thoughtful landscaping, particularly along its grass-covered dam, has resulted in a reservoir that blends in well with its wild surroundings.

Submerged beneath the waters of the lake lies a chapel. There is a memorial to this lost place of worship along the northern shore not far from the road. The modernistic Capel Celyn Memorial, 'designed to resemble a ship coming in from the waters', is built from some of the stones of the original chapel. The memorial also contains three beautifully carved slate tablets bearing the names, dwellings and dates of those buried beneath the lake. Headstones from the original chapel can be seen in a small garden of remembrance nearby.

The rushing river Tryweryn just below the dam is a challenging white-water canoe slalom course.

There are lofty viewpoints across the lake from car parks along the B4518, which runs above Llyn Clywedog's northern shores. To the south, a scenic minor road follows the shores of the lake before entering the Hafren Forest, a large Forestry Commission plantation. An interesting nature trail, with accompanying interpretive material, has been established where the afon (river) Biga emerges from the forest to flow into the western end of the lake. This area, originally marshland, is being developed by introducing native deciduous trees and shrubs and by creating additional water features, all of which can be seen from the trail (which is partly on elevated boardwalks).

Enthusiastic walkers should make for the heart of the Hafren Forest, where one of the trails, over rough wet ground, leads to the source of the river Severn (another famous river, the Wye, also has its source close by).

Bryntail Lead Mine. F. Extensive remains of old mineworkings, where extraction and ore crushing took place, set in Clywedog Gorge. Waymarked trail through site. ⊕

Llyn Clywedog, in the hills above Llanidloes

Machynlleth has one of the most spacious main streets in Wales. Wide Maengwyn Street sweeps along from the town's eastern approaches to the centre, finishing at the base of an elaborate clock tower. Machynlleth is a handsome place, possibly benefiting from the blueprint laid down by 13th-century town planners. Its long main street is lined with tall buildings – some Georgian, others of dark local stone – many of which are attractive shops. Behind this main thoroughfare, Machynlleth's air of spaciousness is maintained by a parkland of open, green fields.

Owain Glyndŵr Centre

Machynlleth's ornate clock tower

The clock tower is Machynlleth's main talking point. This ornamental – perhaps overly ornamental – structure was put up by the Marquess of London-derry in 1873 to mark the coming-of-age of his heir, Lord Castlereagh. The Marquess's grand home, Plas Machynlleth, stands in the nearby parkland. The Plas, a fine 17th-century house, now serves as a centre for local government. The Wynnstay Hotel, in the shadow of the clock tower, is a historic hostelry, its pedigree as a coaching inn plainly evident in its arched entrance. Modern Machynlleth is repre-sented by the recently opened Bro Dyfi Centre, an excellently equipped sports and leisure complex in the park behind the hotel.

At the other end of Maengwyn Street is the Parliament House and Owain Glyndŵr Centre. Glyndŵr, a romantic figure and great folk hero, led a rising against English rule in 1404. For a time he was able to hold Welsh parliaments, one of which is said to have assembled here (Parliament House, as it

now stands, dates from the late 1400s and is much restored). The mercurial Glyndŵr vanished in 1412, never to be seen again.

You can learn all about Owain Glyndŵr in a centre dedicated to him at the Parliament House. Alongside is the Dyfi Centre, which combines tourist information with displays on many aspects of local life and history, including slate quarrying, railways, religion, seafaring and wildlife.

The National Centre for Alternative Technology is located in forested hills to the north of Machynlleth. Established in the unpromising location of a disused slate quarry in the 1970s, this dedicated community has since lived a life based on the principles of conservation and care for the earth's resources, creating a successful 'village of the future' which anticipated the growing concern for 'green' and environmental issues. All kinds of ingenious, energy-saving devices are on show, including wind and water turbines, solar panels and low-energy dwellings.

Bro Dyfi Leisure Centre. Tel (0654) 703300. C. Leisure pool, squash, indoor bowls – even a simulated rock face with climbing for beginners and experts.

Dyfi Centre. Tel (0654) 702401. F. Part of the Tourist Information Centre. Attractively presented displays on local customs, heritage and wildlife.

(contd overleaf)

Open-air shopping at Machynlleth's street market

Owain Glyndŵr Centre, Parliament House.
Tel (0654) 702827. F. Models, photographs,
documents and books depicting Welsh history in
the Middle Ages and Glyndŵr's stand for independence. Also contains a brass rubbing room (C).

Y Tabernacl Cultural Centre. Tel (0654) 703355. C
(for performances). Old chapel converted into arts
centre.

Nearby
Felin Crewi, Penegoes. Tel (0654) 703113. C.
Restored 17th-century watermill producing
wholewheat flour. See the traditional process for
yourself. Riverside walk and nature trail.

National Centre for Alternative Technology (2½
miles north of Machynlleth signposted off A487).
Tel (0654) 702400. C. A world of green living. Energy
conservation, organic gardens, Britain's best
insulated house, water-balanced cliff railway
(scheduled to open summer 1991).

Solar power panels provide energy at the National
Centre for Alternative Technology

MALLWYD
GWYNEDD   D2

This hamlet stands at the foot of steep, green slopes
dedicated to hill sheep farming and forestry.
Mallwyd is an old settlement with lurid associations:
it used to be notorious for its band of red-headed
robbers, who terrorized travellers in Tudor times.
The Brigands' Inn is named after them. Today,
Mallwyd is a quaint hamlet steeped in rural
tranquillity, with two rows of picturesque cottages,
an ancient church dedicated to St Tydecho, and a
Victorian Methodist chapel.

The church porch is interesting. The date 1641
appears over the door (although the building is
much older than that) and so does the rib cage of a
prehistoric animal – possibly a whale or a mammoth
– which was found nearby.

The original church on the site was founded in
the year AD525 and the present building has a
lovely roof of curved oak (known as a canopy of
honour) over the chancel, dating from the 17th
century. It was put there by Dr John Davies, who was
rector for 30 years and one of the first men to
translate the Bible into Welsh.

MONTGOMERY
POWYS   F3

The gnarled shell of Montgomery Castle looks down
from its rocky perch on to a pretty little borderland
town graced with fine Georgian architecture.
Montgomery's delightful town square is lined with
pristine red-bricked buildings which display the
harmonious proportions characteristic of the
Georgian period.

When wandering around this compact place, you
might wonder if the description 'town' is perhaps a
little generous; Montgomery, no larger than a
village, was given town status in a charter of 1227.
The charter came because of the castle, built as a
key border fortress in 1223 to guard the Severn
valley as it enters the Welsh hills, the main approach
from Shrewsbury. In the more peaceful 14th century
the castle played a manorial rather than military
role, though it was back in the wars again during
the 17th-century Civil War, after which it was
demolished by order of Parliament. There are,
nevertheless, interesting remains here – and it is
worth the climb to the top for the views alone.
Another prominent hill above the town is occupied
by the Iron Age fort of Ffridd Faldwyn.

Montgomery's church, mainly of the 13th century,
has a noteworthy double screen and loft. The
churchyard contains the Robber's Grave. John
Davies, hanged in 1821 for sheep stealing, protested
his innocence by predicting that no grass would
grow on his grave for 100 years. According to
records, his prophesy came true.

Montgomery Castle. F. Large twin-towered
gatehouse, impressive rock-cut ditch and 67m-
(220ft-) deep well survive amongst the ruins.
Tremendous views from this commanding spot. ✦

Old Bell Museum. C. Local history centre which
illustrates life of town through the ages. Housed in
16th-century building.

Ruined Montgomery Castle

Sandy cove, tiny church and towering headland at Mwnt

MWNT

DYFED   **B5**

Twenty-five years ago, only a handful of people ever found their way to Mwnt. But with the increase in car ownership, visitors began to discover this enchanting spot on the Cardigan Bay coast. The good news is that Mwnt is as pretty as ever, thanks to the foresight of the National Trust in acquiring this stretch of coast and protecting it from any unsympathetic development. Mwnt also lies on one of Cardigan Bay's stretches of protected Heritage Coast.

Mwnt is a perfect little crescent of sand which shelters beneath a grassy headland. For once, the hyperbole of the holiday brochures is accurate: Mwnt really is the 'jewel of Cardigan Bay'. A solitary little church, dazzling in its coat of whitewash, stands above the beach. The Church of the Holy Cross, solid, stone built and austere, has stood here since medieval times, and may well occupy a religious settlement dating from the dawn of Christianity in Wales.

Once, there were darker forces at work in this idyllic spot. Until a few centuries ago, the first Sunday in January was marked with the game Sul Coch y Mwnt (The Bloody Sunday of the Mound) to commemorate the violent defeat of Flemish landing here in 1155.

NANT-Y-MOCH RESERVOIR

DYFED   **D3**

The dark waters of Nant-y-moch flood high, boggy moorlands on the slopes of the Plynlimon mountain range. Nant-y-moch's waters are held back by a buttressed stone dam, a formidable structure 52m (172ft) high and 351m (1150ft) long which traps the headwaters of the river Rheidol, forming a crescent-shaped lake 3 miles in length. These waters are used to generate energy by powering hydro-electric turbines. In conjunction with the smaller Dinas reservoir a few miles down the valley, they provide the power for the Rheidol Hydro-electric Scheme (see Aberystwyth entry).

The bleak mountains above Nant-y-moch do not peak at a pronounced, easily identifiable summit. Plynlimon's heights have a misleading consistency that almost makes them appear flat, until you remember that they rise to over 750m (2460ft). Summit spotters will have difficulty in picking out the peak, which hides amongst dark crags to the east of the reservoir.

One of Mid Wales's many scenic mountain roads begins at Ponterwyd, running north past the Dinas reservoir to Nant-y-Moch. The road crosses the dam before following the western shores of the lake and dropping down a beautiful valley to Talybont, on the A487 between Aberystwyth and Machynlleth.

NEWCASTLE EMLYN ℹ️
DYFED
B5

The traditional market town of Newcastle Emlyn

Newcastle Emlyn is a flourishing little country and market town with plenty of inns and a good range of shops. It once stood on the boundary between the old counties of Carmarthenshire and Cardiganshire and still has an air of importance unrelated to its size.

The place is full of character, with fascinating byways and some interesting architecture: fine town houses where local dignitaries lived in style are now banks; a Victorian Town Hall in Market Place with a picturesque clock tower; and Bethel Chapel, built near the parish church in 1820, a good example of chapel architecture of that period.

One of the most attractive features of the town is the variety of river views it offers. Some of the best of these can be obtained from the castle ruins, a short walk from Market Place. Here one can clearly see how the town has been built above a broad loop in the river Teifi, bordering a valley which is a serene patchwork of woods and meadows.

Newcastle Emlyn Castle. F. Scanty ruins of the 'new' castle of 1240. Parts of the gatehouse and a few walls remaining on a grassy knoll.

The town grew up alongside a medieval castle

Nearby
Felin Geri, Cwm-cou (off B4333 a mile or so north-west of Newcastle Emlyn). Tel (0239) 710810. C. Variety of attractions in 16 hectares (40 acres) of river scenery centred around a working 16th-century watermill producing stoneground flour. Bakery, sawmill, fishing museum, falconry centre showing various hoods, bells and other equipment, falconry displays, adventure fort for children, craft shop.

Museum of the Welsh Woollen Industry, Dre-fach Felindre (off A484 3 miles south-east of Newcastle Emlyn). Tel (0559) 370929. F. Interpretive centre with craft workshops and operational woollen mill on site. Extensive collection of tools and equipment, including spinning mules and carding engines. 🏭

Teifi Valley Railway, Henllan (3 miles east of Newcastle Emlyn on A484). Tel (0559) 371077. C. Steam and diesel trains run 1½ miles along narrow-gauge line through woodland. Tiny engine shed open to public. Playgrounds, nature trail, amphitheatre.

Falconry display at Felin Geri

NEW/OLD RADNOR
POWYS
F4

New Radnor is actually a Norman settlement, once centred around a castle, whose site can still be seen on a hill above the High Street. Now bypassed by the A44, this is a peaceful place, set on the edge of Radnor Forest's wooded hills and high moorland, originally a hunting ground. New Radnor's most striking and unexpected landmark is an extravagant neo-Gothic memorial, built in 1863, to 'her most distinguished son', politician and statesman George Cornewall Lewis.

The parish church of Old Radnor stands 256m (840ft) above sea level, looking out over the hills 2 miles to the east of New Radnor. It was rebuilt on the site of an earlier place of worship in the 15th and 16th centuries, and has a huge stone font, unusually designed with four hefty feet and probably dating from the 8th century. The church's medieval features include a graceful carved rood screen, ornately lettered floor tiles, and a 1500 organ case, said to be the oldest in Britain.

Along the banks of the Wye

High on Cader Idris

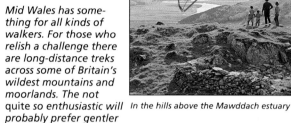

In the hills above the Mawddach estuary

Mid Wales has something for all kinds of walkers. For those who relish a challenge there are long-distance treks across some of Britain's wildest mountains and moorlands. The not quite so enthusiastic will probably prefer gentler hill and lakeside rambles, while families can follow easy waymarked footpaths which steer well clear of the rocks and bottomless bogs of Mid Wales's highlands.

Anyone contemplating a spot of serious walking in Mid Wales should get hold of a copy of George Borrow's Wild Wales. This classic 19th-century book captures the elemental appeal of untamed landscapes. Borrow found some of the wildest country in the Plynlimon mountain range near Ponterwyd (the village's inn was renamed the George Borrow Hotel in honour of the author, who stayed here after a particularly gruelling plod across the moors).

The spirit of Borrow's Wild Wales lives on in this region, as anyone who has walked the Glyndŵr Way, a 123-mile highland route from Knighton to Welshpool via Machynlleth, will readily confirm. Knighton features in many walking guides, for it is also the midway point along the 168-mile Offa's Dyke Path, which runs the length of the Wales/England border. Some of the best stretches of this path – and best-preserved sections of the ancient earthen dyke on which it is based – are to be found in the rolling hills around Knighton.

Another long-distance route follows the lovely Dovey valley deep into the mountains –

you can walk up one side of the valley from Aberdovey to Llanuwchllyn, and down the other side back to the sea at Borth, a distance of 108 miles. Rhayader is the starting point of the Wye Valley Walk, which runs southwards through splendid hill and river scenery.

Long-distance paths are just one feature of Mid Wales's varied walking scene. You can walk almost anywhere in this region – along estuaries and dunelands, through forests and nature reserves, beside lakes and waterfalls. And you can choose the kind of walk that you feel comfortable with, even if it's just a half-hour stroll. Call in at a Tourist Information Centre for advice on local walks and trails, together with details of any guided walks that may be available.

The Offa's Dyke Path follows ancient earthworks, the first border between Wales and England

New Quay's attractive harbour maintains a traditional appearance

NEW QUAY

DYFED   B4

There's a strong tang of Cardigan Bay's salty old seafaring days at picturesque New Quay. A list of the old 'tolls and duties to be levied on ships and vessels' landing goods at the harbour remains on display outside the harbourmaster's office. The notice states that a ton of coal attracted a charge of four pence (old money, of course), a box of French plums two pence, a bath chair one shilling, and a coffin two shillings. The list of tolls includes all kinds of goods – everything from soap to coconuts – an inventory which tells us a great deal about life along the Welsh coast before the coming of railways and proper roads.

Lobster boats still work out of the harbour, though these are now outnumbered by pleasure craft. The sheltered harbour and beach, tucked in tight behind New Quay Head, are well insulated from the westerly winds. Dylan Thomas's imaginary seatown of Llareggub (you'll get the joke if you spell it backwards), the setting for his famous 'play for voices' *Under Milk Wood*, bears more than a passing resemblance to New Quay. The writer first conceived of the idea for the play when he was living here, and the town certainly matches his description of 'cliff-perched terraces at the far end of Wales'.

The steep hillside above the harbour is lined with prim terraces and straight-laced Victorian villas. Verandahs, bay windows and even the odd tea room are all signs of a small seaside town which cares little for fashion, and is all the more charming for it.

New Quay's long, sandy beach, which sweeps around in an arc from the harbour, is a popular spot in summer. A mile or so to the north-east is Cei Bach,

a quieter beach which is not so easily accessible (park at the clifftop car park then follow the path down to the sands). In the opposite direction, a spectacular coast path – beware of the steep drops! – leads around New Quay Head and across the cliffs to Bird's Rock (which has one of the largest sea-bird colonies in these parts) and a coastguard look-out point. If you continue on this path you'll come to Cwm Tudu, a tiny secluded beach (also accessible by minor road) which occupies a break in the cliffs. This sand and pebble cove, once a haunt of smugglers, is in a beautiful 'off-the-beaten-track' location and a good place from which to explore stretches of Cardigan Bay's Heritage Coast.

Secluded Cwm Tudu

If the railway boom of the 19th century had reached Newtown a little earlier, it could have developed into a place of dark, satanic mills, rather than the lively rural market town and commercial centre which it has now become. Nevertheless, textiles were an important part of Newtown's history. Warehouses and weaving sheds recall the town's past as a centre of the busy textile industry when it was known as 'the Leeds of Wales'. The grandiose façades of buildings such as Barclays Bank and Pryce-Jones, Mid Wales's biggest department store, are legacies of the wealth which weaving brought to the region from the 1790s to the 1930s.

Newtown's W H Smith is a period piece

Newtown avoided a decline into faded anonymity, gaining fresh life from its apt designation as a 'new town' after World War II. Nowadays two modern shopping malls complement the large Victorian market on High Street, and a promenade provides pleasant walking beside the river Severn. The industry which made such a lasting mark is recalled in the Textile Factory in Commercial Street, which takes up the two upper floors of an 1820 row of houses, built with enough space for 22 weaving looms. A fascinating exhibition includes sewing machines and 100-year-old woollen clothes, in perfect condition.

In the centre of town several interesting architectural styles crowd the main shopping streets, including the ornate Barclays clock tower and a brick-and-timber W H Smith, restored to its early 20th-century elegance and housing a small exhibition about the famous firm on its upper floor. Older buildings can be seen in the side streets and squares leading towards the river.

About 3 miles north-east of Newtown, along twisting, narrow lanes off the A483 near Abermule, are the remains of Dolforwyn Castle, a Welsh fortress built by Llywelyn ap Gruffudd in 1273.

Davies Memorial Gallery. Tel (0686) 625041. F. Temporary exhibitions of paintings and crafts in modern annexe near new Town Hall.

Newtown Textile Museum, 5,6 and 7 Commercial Street (ask at no 7 for the key). F. History of the woollen industry, with looms, wool samples and reconstructed corner shop. Photo display of local 'characters'.

Robert Owen Memorial Museum, Broad Street. F. Original furnishings from Owen's birthplace.

Theatr Hafren, Llanidloes Road. Tel (0686) 625007. Varied programme of opera, drama and dance.

(contd overleaf)

Newtown stands amongst rolling border country

It was from the factories of Newtown that the co-operative movement grew, initiated by the town's most famous son, Robert Owen. His experimental village in New Lanark earned him the title 'Father of Socialism', and the Robert Owen Museum on the corner of Broad and Severn Streets reconstructs his home, originally on the top floor of the building which is now the Midland Bank. Owen is buried in the churchyard of St Mary's, a ruin set in quiet gardens. The church itself, whose 13th-century tower is still intact, served the parish for 500 years until disrepair, lack of space and regular flooding forced the congregation to abandon it in 1856. The gates of the churchyard were a gift from Robert Owen's children in 1858. St David's, which took over St Mary's role, stands in New Road opposite a palatial Baptist church.

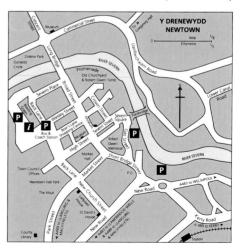

**W H Smith Museum, High Street. Tel (0686) 626280.
F. Photographs and models tracing growth of
famous stationery firm.**

**Nearby
Dolforwyn Castle. F. Remains of stronghold built by
Welsh leader Llywelyn the Last, gradually being
excavated.** ✿

PAINSCASTLE
POWYS   F5

Sleepy Painscastle, deep in the heart of undisturbed
border country, was not always so tranquil.
Although little now remains of the early 12th-
century fortress which gave this village its name, a
visit still gives you a clear impression of the castle's
strategic advantages. Large, overgrown mounds,
where horses graze, map out the area of the motte
and bailey, which would once have towered over
the tiny village. From this site in the heart of the
Marches there are sweeping views of the surrounding fields and hills – invaluable in the days of
constant conflict between Norman and Welsh forces.

Outside the Post Office there's an oddity which
survives from the days before the invention of the
motor car – a small flight of steps used as a block to
mount horses.

PENMAENPOOL
GWYNEDD   D2

The George III at Penmaenpool

The Victorian poet Gerard Manley Hopkins wrote a
poem about this lovely spot on the Mawddach
estuary and inscribed it in the visitors' book of the
local inn. The waterside George III Hotel still
welcomes guests who are invariably impressed with
the timeless beauty of its surroundings. You can
enjoy a peaceful drink while gazing across the
estuary to the oak woodland on the far side, or
stroll along the path the local railway used to
follow.

The railway closed in 1965 but ingenious use has
been made of its relics. The one-time waiting room
and stationmaster's house have now been incorpo-
rated into the hotel and the signal box has been

converted into a Royal Society for the Protection of
Birds observation post.

A timber toll bridge crosses the estuary here, a
handy short cut which avoids Dolgellau.

**Penmaenpool Wildlife Centre. F. A treat for all
nature lovers. Telescopes and binoculars are
provided in this one-time signal box, now a vantage
point for birdwatchers. In winter migrants include
ringed plover, oystercatcher, curlew, godwit and
redshank. Lots of free information, including videos
you can sit and watch. A beautiful spot.**

PENRHYNDEUDRAETH
GWYNEDD   C1

This unpretentious small town stands on the busy
A487 between Maentwrog and Porthmadog. It
provides access to the toll road across the mouth of
the river Dwyryd, which cuts miles off the journey to
or from Harlech. The street leading down to the toll
road has a viewpoint over the estuary. There's an
unexpected choice of small shops on the Beddgelert
road out of town. The entrance to the unique
Italianate village of Portmeirion, creation of the
architect Sir Clough Williams-Ellis, is on the A487 on
the western approach to the town (see Portmeirion
entry).

PONTERWYD
POWYS   D3

Although Ponterwyd straddles the busy A44
between Llangurig and Aberystwyth, it can still
conjure up the *Wild Wales* written about so
compellingly by traveller George Borrow in the
1850s. The inn where he found shelter from the
elements is now the George Borrow Hotel, offering
modern comforts to hikers and tourists. But there is
a frontier feel to the village even today, due mainly
to the windswept solitudes of the Cambrian
Mountains which surround it. This is high country:
the river Rheidol, which flows through the middle of

Water power at the Llywernog Silver-Lead Mine

Ponterwyd, drops 533m (1750ft) in only 28 miles from its nearby source on the western side of Plynlimon to the sea, making it one of Britain's fastest-flowing rivers.

The barrenness of this area was once seen as a promise of wealth. Miners were drawn here by the belief that the gases given off by lead ore prevented the growth of vegetation, and traces of lead-mining activity go back to prehistoric days. There was plenty of lead to be found and the boom years of the late 19th century saw the extraction of thousands of tons of the ore. Another particular attraction for the miners in this region was the lead's impurity: it contained silver. At the Llywernog Silver-Lead Mining Museum, a mile west of Ponterwyd, you can follow a miners' trail through a site which operated from 1740 to 1914. This private museum was set up in the 1970s to record one out of countless mineworkings which appeared and disappeared here over the centuries.

A little further west again, at the edge of the Cambrians, there's a superb view of a more fertile landscape. From the Bwlch Nant-yr-Arian Visitor Centre you can see wooded mountains and lush valleys stretching down to Cardigan Bay. The centre serves as an introduction to the Forestry Commission's Rheidol Forest. Walks from the centre include a 1½-mile forest trail along an old lead mine leat; and the 5-mile Jubilee Walk, which leads to two small lakes at Pendam. Look out for the 3m (10ft) 'sculpture in the mountains', *Side-Step*, made from laminated Douglas Fir by Stephen Collingbourne.

Nearby
Bwlch Nant-yr-Arian Visitor Centre (off A44 2½ miles west of Ponterwyd): contact Forest District Manager, tel (09743) 404. F. Exhibition on local wildlife, history and forest; walks, picnic sites.

Llywernog Silver-Lead Mining Museum (off A44 1 mile west of Ponterwyd). Tel (0970) 85620. C. Self-guided footpath through restored mining site. Includes giant wheel-pit and workshops, plus exhibition.

PONTRHYDFENDIGAID
DYFED   D4

This grey-stoned village, standing alone on an upland plain, is a Welsh community steeped in cultural and religious traditions. Each May, it hosts a well-attended eisteddfod. Modest Pontrhydfendigaid is able to accommodate large numbers thanks to the generosity of a local man, Sir David John James, who made his fortune in London and built the cavernous pavilion on the edge of the village which seats 3000.

This area has attracted outside interest since medieval times. In the foothills of the Cambrian Mountains 1 mile south-east of the village lie the ruins of Strata Florida Abbey, in its prime the 'Westminster Abbey of Wales'. Strata Florida (its name is a latinized version of the Welsh ystrad fflur, meaning 'the way of the flowers') was founded by Cistercian monks in the 12th century. Their abbey became much more than a religious house. It was a

Strata Florida's decorative archway

centre of great political, cultural and educational influence in medieval Wales; its enterprising monks are even credited with introducing new agricultural methods, and became successful sheep farmers.

Strata Florida's evocative remnants, surrounded by silent farmlands, contain the occasional reminder of the abbey's former status – most notably, its decorative Romanesque archway and sections of mosaic tiled floor. Many of Wales's native rulers are believed to be buried here. The celebrated 14th-century poet, Dafydd ap Gwilym, is said to rest under the gnarled old yew tree in the adjoining churchyard.

This churchyard also contains many graves of those who worked in the local lead mines. On a lighter note, see if you can spot the grave of Henry Hughes Cooper – it's the one with a small headstone decorated with an amputated leg! All is revealed in the inscription, which reads: 'The left leg and part of the thigh of Henry Hughes Cooper was cut off and intern'd here June 18th 1756.' Where the rest of poor Henry was buried remains a mystery.

A minor road leading east from Ffair-rhos just north of Pontrhydfendigaid ends up beside the lonely Teifi Pools, mountain lakes which form the headwaters of one of the loveliest rivers in Wales.

Strata Florida Abbey. Tel (09745) 261. C. Ruins of one of Wales's most important religious communities. ✪

PONTRHYDYGROES
DYFED   D4

Tranquillity is the main attraction of this scenic spot on the wooded hills above the Ystwyth. Thick forests of broadleaved trees and conifers spread down the steep sides of the valley, on land which once formed part of the Hafod estate. It was here that Thomas

WELSH WORDS EXPLAINED

Welsh placenames can tell us a lot about the town, village, area or mountain in question. Many Welsh placenames are based on local physical or geographic features, such as rivers, hills, bridges, woodlands and so on. Aber, for example, means 'mouth of', so Aberaeron means 'The mouth of the river Aeron'.

Here are a few examples of Welsh names you'll come across on your travels:

aber	confluence, rivermouth
afon	river
bach, fach	small
ban, fan	peak, crest
blaen	head, end, source
bryn	hill
bwlch	pass ·
caer, gaer	fort, stronghold
carreg	stone, rock
castell	castle
cefn	ridge
clawdd	hedge, ditch, dyke
coch, goch	red
craig, graig	rock
crib	crest, summit, ridge
cwm	valley, cirque
cymer	meeting of rivers
dinas	fort, city
du, ddu	black
dyffryn	valley
eglwys	church
ffin	boundary
glyn	glen
gwaun, waen	moor, mountain pasture
hendre	winter dwelling, permanent home

heol	road
llan	church, enclosure
llwyn	grove, bush
llyn	lake
llys	hall, court
maen	stone
mawr, fawr	great, big
merthyr	church, burial place
moel, foel	bare hill
mynydd, fynydd	mountain, moorland
pant	hollow, valley
pen	head, top, end
pentre	village, homestead
plas	hall, mansion
pont, bont	bridge
sarn	causeway, old road
tre, tref	hamlet, home, town
uchaf	upper, higher, highest
ystrad	valley floor

A FEW GREETINGS

bore da	good morning
dydd da	good day
prynhawn da	good afternoon
noswaith dda	good evening
nos da	good night
sut mae?	how are you?
hwyl	cheers
diolch	thanks
diolch yn fawr iawn	thanks very much
croeso	welcome
croeso i Gymru	welcome to Wales
da	good
da iawn	very good
iechyd da!	good health!

Johnes pioneered the work of afforesting the hills, planting six million trees from 1780 to 1813, to counter the fact that 'great digging for leade . . . hath destroid the woodes'. Guests were entertained in lavish style at Johnes's mansion, Hafod Uchtryd, and his library housed an impressive collection of Welsh manuscripts. House and library were burned down in 1807, and although he rebuilt his home, Johnes never managed to recreate the atmosphere of Hafod Uchtryd. The new version was eventually demolished in 1962.

On the B4574 to Cwm Ystwyth a gateway on the right of the road leads down the hill to Hafod Church, which has marvellous views over the Ystwyth valley towards the Cambrian Mountains. A little further along, where the B4574 loops north-westwards from Cwm Ystwyth to Devil's Bridge, the road runs under a pointed stone arch. This is another Johnes creation, built in 1810 to mark George III's Golden Jubilee. Three waymarked trails through the conifers of the Ystwyth Forest begin at the arch.

PORTMEIRION
GWYNEDD   C1

Portmeirion is one of the few places that almost defies description. The visual extravagance of this fantasy village eclipses all attempts to pin it down in words. Eccentric, strange, charming, bizarre, amusing, disorienting . . . these are just some of the impressions which visitors to this unique place come away with. This would have pleased Portmeirion's creator, architect and iconoclast Sir Clough Williams-Ellis, who built the village piecemeal over the years between 1925 and 1972.

Portmeirion, which nestles on a wooded hillside on its own little peninsula overlooking a dreamy view of sand, sea and mountain, is much more redolent of southern Italy than North Wales. Sir Clough's village consists of colour-washed buildings, fountains, statues, columns, and fake façades that front nothing. Look closer at his various creations and you will discover an amazing combination of

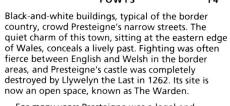

Black-and-white buildings, typical of the border country, crowd Presteigne's narrow streets. The quiet charm of this town, sitting at the eastern edge of Wales, conceals a lively past. Fighting was often fierce between English and Welsh in the border areas, and Presteigne's castle was completely destroyed by Llewelyn the Last in 1262. Its site is now an open space, known as The Warden.

For many years Presteigne was a legal and administrative centre, conducting Radnorshire's Quarter Sessions and Assizes until 1970. The courts were held at Shire Hall, a grand, pillared building on Broad Street. A small museum is now based here, describing the area's past life.

A gravestone in St Andrew's Church marks the burial in 1805 of Mary Morgan, a 17-year-old sentenced to hang for the murder of a newborn illegitimate child, by a jury which included the baby's father. A reprieve was obtained from London but was too late to save the girl. Facing the original gravestone, which describes her as a 'victim of sin and shame', is a second stone, erected by the people of Presteigne, and engraved: 'He that is without sin among you, let him first cast a stone at her.' The church itself is worth seeing for the 16th-century Flemish tapestry which is on display there. A nightly curfew is still rung from the church's 13th-century tower.

A walk around the town reveals some fine old buildings, such as the Radnorshire Arms, built in 1616, and Radnor Buildings, whose ornamental plasterwork and mosaics make it an impressive landmark. Lugg Bridge marks the point where England meets Wales; and near the river, reached from Mill Lane, is the Withybeds Nature Reserve, 1 hectare (2$\frac{1}{2}$ acres) of protected woodland.

Italy meets Wales at Portmeirion

different architectural styles and influences – everything from oriental to traditional English – reflecting Sir Clough's 'gay, light-opera sort of approach'.

The location for this magic place is perfect: surrounding the village on three sides are sub-tropical woodlands, criss-crossed by miles of paths leading to beaches of gleaming sand.

Portmeirion's ambiguous character and other-worldly atmosphere came to the fore, of course, when the village achieved massive exposure as the setting for that cult 1960s television series, *The Prisoner*, starring Patrick McGoohan. *Prisoner* fans still make the pilgrimage to this surreal spot to relive scenes from the series' baffling story line.

Portmeirion. Tel (0766) 770228. C. The most un-Welsh village in Wales. Has the atmosphere of a strange, self-contained world. In a beautiful location.

Dazzling sands along Portmeirion's little peninsula

When the mists hang around the high country in which this hamlet is located, there are those who are inclined, uncharitably, to say that they fully understand where Staylittle got its unusual name from. The name derives, in fact, from the legend of a local blacksmith who was so good at his job that travellers had to 'stay little' while he attended to the shoes of their horses.

Staylittle stands in exposed, empty highlands which have their fair share of inclement weather; but the elemental nature of these surroundings defines Staylittle's appeal. Some of Wales's most uncompromising wilderness areas lie on its doorstep. The vast Hafren Forest blankets the hills to the west. A huge waterfall plummets down from nearby Dylife (see entry). And on a fine day – yes, the weather can often be kind in these mountains, despite their rainy reputation – there's nothing better than a walk along the grassy lakesides at nearby Llyn Clywedog (see entry).

Meet the locals at one of Rhayader's many old inns

Rhayader is a busy little crossroads town in the heart of the Welsh hills. The A470 north–south road meets the east–west A44 at Rhayader's neat little clock tower. The town offers visitors a glimpse into the commercial side of Welsh farming: it holds one of the leading livestock markets in Mid Wales, its regular sales of sheep, cattle and ponies swelling the population of the town (not to mention the numbers that patronize its characterful old inns) to bursting point. Market day is Wednesday.

Architecturally, the town is unremarkable. Rhayader's appeal lies in its friendly atmosphere, superb location and the excellent range of outdoor pursuits available locally. The town, which stands at the approach to the lovely Elan valley lakelands (see entry), is surrounded by some of Wales's most spectacular touring country – follow the mountain road to Cwm Ystwyth and Devil's Bridge, for example, or explore the gentle hills of the border country around Radnor and Knighton.

Rhayader is the first town on the river Wye, so good fishing is guaranteed. Pony trekking is something of a local speciality, with a choice of centres offering everything from a half-day in the saddle to a full week's trekking. The town is also a good mountain biking centre, while walkers can head for the hills or follow leafy riverside paths (Rhayader is at the start of the long-distance Wye Valley Walk).

Gigrin Farm Trail (signposted on southern approach to town). Tel (0597) 810243. C. Walk through a typical working Welsh hill farm. Children's playground, picnic site.

Marston Pottery, Lower Cefn Faes (³/₄ mile north of town centre). Tel (0597) 810875. F. Distinctively coloured hand-thrown stoneware. Wide range of pots. Pottery courses. In attractive setting.

Rhayader Museum. F. Small local museum reflecting everyday life in bygone days.

This small village hugs the A496 between Harlech and Maentwrog. The tiny church has a steep slate roof and bellcote. Fine views across the Traeth Bach estuary can be enjoyed by going down the lane that leads to the railway station. Park by the station, walk across the level crossing – don't attempt to drive over – and continue down the lane to reach an expanse of fenland, which you can cross to reach the sands of Traeth Bach. It is, however, a fair walk and families with young children can find far more accessible beaches around Harlech and Porthmadog.

This is a tranquil spot looking towards the Italianate fantasy village of Portmeirion (see entry) on the opposite shore, its colour-washed towers peeping out from thick woodlands against the mountainous backdrop of Snowdonia.

Snowdonia from the hills above Talsarnau

Tal-y-llyn lies deep in the folds of the mountains

TALYBONT

GWYNEDD **C2**

Talybont is a leafy village where the older cottages have been supplemented by new bungalows. The river Ysgethin rushes down from the mountains to flow beneath a stone bridge. A sandy beach backed by a shingle ridge and dunes is 1200m (³/₄ mile) away. To reach it, turn left just before entering the village from the south.

Talybont Museum of Transport and Rural Life. Tel (03417) 7705. C. Over-50s will remember these objects; younger people will find them enthralling. Famous old street ads – including the Bisto Kids – Dinky toys, steamrollers, vintage cars and bikes. Re-creation of village stores, wireless shop and so on.

TAL-Y-LLYN LAKE

GWYNEDD **D2**

This 1-mile-long lake, directly beneath the rocky summit of Cader Idris, lies in a deep valley formed by a major geological fault and the action of Ice Age glaciers. The B4405 runs along the southern shores, offering memorable views of lake and mountainside as the rocky screes of Cader Idris plunge down into the sheltered valley.

A well-known path to the top of Cader Idris starts at Minffordd a short distance up the valley from the head of the lake. The path climbs past waterfalls and through a nature reserve based around the cliff-backed mountain lake of Llyn Cau before reaching the 892m (2927ft) summit.

TRAWSFYNYDD

GWYNEDD **D1**

The mountain village of Trawsfynydd lies just off the main road between Dolgellau and Maentwrog. It's a place of quiet dignity, with well-maintained stone terraces and an away-from-it-all feeling. It was the

home of Hedd Wyn, a shepherd-poet killed at Flanders just before he would have received the chief bardic prize at the National Eisteddfod of 1917 (held, interestingly, at Birkenhead – in those days this great festival was sometimes held outside Wales). The award to Hedd Wyn was made posthumously and his statue stands in the centre of the village, outside Moriah Chapel.

The lake beside the village provides the cooling waters for the Trawsfynydd Nuclear Power Station, located a mile or so to the north. Overlooking the lake on moorland to the east of the A470 is Tomen-y-Mur (no direct access), a Roman fort whose defences were added to by the Normans.

Nearby
Rhiw Goch Ski Centre, Bronaber. Tel (076687) 578. C. Dry slope skiing for beginners and experts, 305m (1000ft) above sea level in Snowdonia National Park. Main run 100m (328ft) long, nursery slope 17m (55ft). Holiday village close by.

Trawsfynydd Nuclear Power Station. Tel (076687) 331. F. See how electricity is made on a guided tour of Britain's only inland nuclear power station.

Rhiw Goch Ski Centre

59

TREGARON
DYFED   **D4**

Fresh produce for sale at Tregaron

There's a no-nonsense charm to this small, Welsh-speaking market town on a tributary of the river Teifi. Despite its size, it has produced several celebrated sons. One is recalled in the name Tregaron, which means 'Home of Caron', a reference to the 3rd-century King of Ceredigion. Twm Siôn Cati, a legendary and romanticized outlaw in the Robin Hood mould, was also born here, as was Henry Richard, the 'Apostle of Peace' who founded the Peace Union, forerunner of the League of Nations. A statue of Richard stands in the compact central square, where you can find a well-stocked shop and gallery known as the Craft Design Centre of Wales. This square was the place where drovers gathered before setting off on their daunting trek across the wilds of the Abergwesyn Pass to markets in England. For one of the most memorable motoring experiences in Britain, drive across this twisting, narrow mountain road to Llanwrtyd Wells.

Tregaron's isolated setting in the Dyfed uplands makes it a useful centre for outdoor activities. Pony trekking is popular here, and there are several good walks from town. This is also spectacular motoring country: in addition to the Abergwesyn Pass, there's a network of county roads leading to beauty spots such as Devil's Bridge, Llyn Brianne and Cwm Ystwyth.

On the outskirts of Tregaron is a strange, flat area of wetland known as Cors Caron (Tregaron Bog), 4 miles of raised peat bog through which the Teifi flows. Now managed by the Nature Conservancy Council, the area attracts a wide variety of birds and sustains bog mosses, deer grass and other wetland vegetation. The only public access without a permit is along an old railway line, now a nature trail, beside the B4343 a few miles north-east of Tregaron.

On the B4577 near the hamlet of Penuwch, the Brimstone Wildlife Centre gives a taste of more exotic flora and fauna. Multi-coloured birds and butterflies flit round visitors' heads in the Tropical House, and a pony and trap makes trips round the park, where there are 2 hectares (5 acres) of wild meadow flowers, as well as an Insectarium and special children's sections, including a Pets' Petting Paddock, Bunnyland and Mouse World.

Craft Design Centre of Wales. Tel (0974) 298415. F. Shop and gallery selling large range of high-quality Welsh handmade products. Welsh woollens centre. Also contains Rhiannon Jewellery, specialists in Celtic designs, some in Welsh gold.

Nearby
Brimstone Wildlife Centre, Brynamlwg, Penuwch. Tel (097423) 439. C. Wildlife and exotic flora and fauna on a hillside setting.

Tregaron Pottery, Castell Flemish (about 3 miles north-west of Tregaron on A485). Tel (097421) 639. F. An attractive and extensive range of stoneware in subtle colours.

TREGYNON
POWYS   **E2**

Gregynog Hall

Tregynon stands in rolling, sleepy farmlands midway between Newtown and Llanfair Caereinion. Its main claim to fame is Gregynog Hall, an impressive black-and-white mansion (you see a lot of half-timbered dwellings in these parts, an indication of cross-border influences). In 1921, Gregynog Hall came into the ownership of the Davies sisters, granddaughters of the wealthy industrialist and philanthropist David Davies of Llandinam (see Llandinam entry). Like their grandfather, they were stern teetotallers, and caused the local pub, The Dragon, to close. The building, renamed The Temperance, still stands at the crossroads.

The sisters were generous patrons of the arts, and left their splendid house and extensive parklands to the University of Wales, which uses it for conferences, meetings and courses. Their magnificent art collection, which is particularly strong in French Impressionist 19th-century paintings, can be seen at the National Museum of Wales, Cardiff.

TRE'R-DDOL
DYFED   C3

The old chapel at Tre'r-ddol on the A487 between Aberystwyth and Machynlleth, closed in the 1870s because it was too small to accommodate its congregation, has been put to good use. It is the home of a wide range of items collected by the late R J Thomas, who purchased Yr Hen Gapel (The Old Chapel) in 1961 and established a museum here. His collection, now part of the National Museum of Wales, reflects 19th-century religious life and Thomas's interests as a collector of all kinds of historical artefacts.

Yr Hen Gapel (The Old Chapel). Tel (0970) 86407. F. Religious and social history on display in 19th-century Wesleyan chapel. 🏛

TYWYN
GWYNEDD   C2

You can make the most of Tywyn's excellent sands; and also take advantage of this long-established resort's excellent location and explore the coast and countryside of the southern Snowdonia National Park. Tywyn is the ideal seaside resort-cum-touring centre. The seaside here is appealingly old fashioned: Tywyn is a straightforward place, with none of the noisy embellishments or bright lights found at other resorts.

The Talyllyn Railway runs into the hills from Tywyn

Beside the sea at Tywyn

The emphasis is on the beach. Tywyn's name means 'sand dune', which gives some indication of the coastal terrain. A vast 3-mile beach – much of it dune-backed – stretches southwards towards Aberdovey, offering good swimming conditions and plenty of space for all. A wide promenade adds to the air of spaciousness.

A long, lively main street links the seafront to the centre of town, where you'll find St Cadfan's Church. This church contains a monument of great antiquity. St Cadfan's Stone is a spindly 2m (7ft) pillar which bears faint traces of what is believed to be the earliest written Welsh, probably dating from the 7th century, which reads, 'The body of Cingen lies beneath'. The stone is a fortunate survivor: it was rescued from a farmer's field where it was used as a gatepost. The church in the village of Llanegryn (see entry) 4 miles to the north-east contains another great treasure, a magnificently carved rood screen, one of the finest in Wales.

Back in Tywyn, every visitor wants to take a ride on the Talyllyn Railway. This narrow-gauge line travels through lovely countryside to the mountain halt of Nant Gwernol near Abergynolwyn, the starting point of a number of waymarked woodland walks (see Abergynolwyn and Dol-goch entries). The Talyllyn, one of the 'Great Little Trains of Wales', was opened in 1865 and has operated continuously ever since. Its station at Tywyn houses a Narrow-Gauge Railway Museum, packed with engines, displays and memorabilia from the days of steam.

Holgates Nutritional Foods. Tel (0654) 711171. F. Shop (part of factory) on outskirts of town with video and displays showing manufacturing process.

Talyllyn Railway and Narrow-Gauge Railway Museum. Tel (0654) 710472. C. Railway runs for 7 miles into the hills. Line originally built to carry slate from Abergynolwyn. Railway museum at the station.

Tywyn Leisure Centre. Tel (0654) 710167. C. Swimming pool, squash, sauna and solarium.

SCENIC DRIVES

Abergwesyn Pass

Bwlch y Groes

Motorists can forget about the frustrations of city driving when they come to Mid Wales. There are no major urban areas to struggle through, no car parking problems, no nose-to-tail convoys. You might drive all day

Above the Mawddach estuary

and not come across a single traffic light in Mid Wales, a region in which the biggest road hazard you're likely to encounter will be the unpredictable behaviour of a dopy sheep.

This is the region for scenic mountain roads and peaceful country lanes. Wales's highest road, the spectacular Bwlch y Groes, climbs up into the mountains from Dinas Mawddwy. Other classic mountain routes include the narrow ribbon of tarmac which runs across high country from Llyn Clywedog to Machynlleth, and the Cwm Ystwyth road from Rhayader to Devil's Bridge.

When it comes to compiling a 'top ten' of great British mountain roads, the route that

winds its way for 14 lonely miles across the wildernesses of Abergwesyn will surely be a front-runner. The Abergwesyn Pass, originally a drovers' road, travels across the 'Roof of Wales' between Tregaron and Llanwrtyd Wells. This undiscovered area has been opened up further by the construction of the Llyn Brianne reservoir and an access road which links up with the pass.

You're spoilt for choice in Mid Wales. Drive along the scenic Mawddach and Dovey estuaries or the cliff-backed coast road that connects the two. Head for the lakelands of the Elan valley, Llyn Clywedog or Nant-y-moch. Explore the maze of roads in rolling, lazy border country around Llandrindod Wells, Knighton and Welshpool.

For further details on the roads mentioned here and the many other scenic routes in Mid Wales, call in at a Tourist Information Centre.

... AND RAIL RIDES

Six narrow-gauge railways operate in Mid Wales – the Fairbourne and Barmouth (see Fairbourne entry), the Welshpool and Llanfair (see Llanfair Caereinion entry), the Talyllyn (see Tywyn entry), the Bala Lake (see Llanuwchllyn entry), the Vale of Rheidol (see Aberystwyth entry) and the Teifi Valley (see Newcastle Emlyn entry). British Rail also has its scenic lines. Take a trip on the cross-country Heart of Wales line through idyllic countryside, or the Cambrian Coast railway that runs northwards along Cardigan Bay from Aberystwyth.

British Rail's scenic Cambrian Coast line

Welshpool's Victorian Town Hall, topped by a grand clock tower, dominates the main street

This pleasant borderland town of wide, well-ordered streets displays influences that are more English than Welsh. Tudor half-timbered, Georgian and red brick are the preferred architectural styles here, a reflection of the town's location at a main entry point into Wales created by the broad valley of the river Severn.

Welshpool's spacious High Street, its main shopping thoroughfare, is full of interesting old buildings – the 15th-/16th-century Buttery and Prentice Traders, for example, which stand side-by-side, and preserve delicately carved, highly patterned timber frontages. It's little wonder that Welshpool has a bustling air. The town is a natural hub of communications, and maintains a long-standing tradition as a marketplace for the area (it was granted a weekly market in a charter of 1263). Market day is Monday.

There's a wealth of fascinating nooks and crannies to seek out in Welshpool. The town has the only cockpit remaining on its original site in Wales.

A hexagonal brick building, dating from the early 18th century, it was used until 1849, when cockfighting was declared illegal.

Welshpool stands on the Montgomery Canal. Its town wharf, consisting of a canal yard and dock basin, has been attractively renovated in recent years. Boat trips along a restored section of the canal depart from the wharf, and the dock warehouse is the home of the Powysland Museum and Montgomery Canal Centre, which displays items on local history and archaeology.

If you are interested in oddities, then it's worth taking a look at Welshpool's British Rail station. This flamboyant 19th-century building – with more than a passing resemblance to a French chateau – was originally designed to serve as a company headquarters as well as mere station. Welshpool's other station, at the opposite end of town, is an altogether more modest affair. It serves the narrow-gauge Welshpool and Llanfair Light Railway, which runs for 8 miles to Llanfair Caereinion (see Llanfair Caereinion entry).

Welshpool has two noteworthy churches. St Mary's stands on high ground overlooking the town. Although dating from the 13th century, the inevitable 19th-century restoration has given the church an elaborate Victorian atmosphere. Look out for the monument to the 2nd Earl of Powis, at whose feet are effigies of a griffon and an elephant, the latter reflecting the family's connections with Clive of India.

Christ Church, west of the town centre, commands fine views across the lush Severn valley. Severely neo-Norman, with needle-sharp towers, its foundation stone was laid on 5 November 1839 to commemorate the 21st birthday of Viscount Clive, heir of Powis.

No mention of Welshpool is complete without referring to Powis Castle, a sumptuous mansion 1 mile south-west of the town (you can walk to it

The old canal basin has been given a new lease of life

Powysland Museum and Montgomery Canal Centre.
Tel (0938) 554656. F. Exhibits mainly based on local history and archaeology.

Welshpool and Llanfair Light Railway. *Tel (0938) 810441. C. One of Wales's 'Great Little Trains'. Main terminus at Llanfair Caereinion.*

Nearby
Moors Collection *(1 mile to the north on the A483). Tel (0938) 553395. C. Collection of farm animals, rare breeds and waterfowl. Pet's corner, picnic area, play area, putting green.*

YNYSLAS

DYFED   C3

There are not many parts of Mid Wales that are as flat as a pancake. The approach to Ynyslas, at the southern mouth of the Dovey estuary, is one. The dunes of the Dyfi National Nature Reserve are the tallest features for miles around in a low lying area of sand and saltmarsh.

This protected habitat supports a wide variety of wildlife. It's an excellent place for birdwatching, especially in winter when the estuary becomes an important refuge for wildfowl and waders. In summer, butterflies are a common sight as they flutter between the colourful plants which grow amongst the dunes.

Powis Castle

through the castle's parklands – the pathway starts just behind the High Street; otherwise take the A483 south and follow the signs). Powis Castle was not always such a grand place. Originally built as a border stronghold, it has evolved over the centuries into a stately, red-stoned mansion. Its interior is graced with such mouth-watering features as a gilded state bedchamber of 1688, though for many, the high point of their visit is the gardens, a staircase of Italianate terraces cut into the steep slope beneath Powis's mock-battlements. Created between 1688 and 1722, they are the only formal gardens of this date in Britain to survive in their original form. A museum within the castle recalls Powis's association with Clive of India.

Powis Castle. Tel (0938) 554336. C. Wealth of fine furniture and paintings. Treasures from India in Clive Museum. Outstanding gardens. 🌿

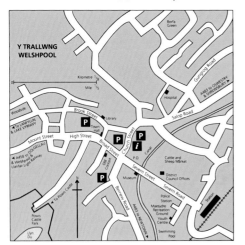

Ynyslas's dunes and beach, on the southern shores of the beautiful Dovey estuary

Ynyslas attracts not only naturalists. This scenic, sandy spot is also popular for its beauty and wide, open spaces. Swimming, though, is unsafe anywhere along the mouth of the estuary – go further south towards Borth (see entry) for safe, gently, shelving beaches.

One of Mid Wales's classic views can be enjoyed from Ynyslas's sands by looking northwards across the waters to Aberdovey, whose colourful waterfront houses huddle in a long line below steep, green mountainsides.

Ynyslas Visitor Centre. Tel (0970) 871640. F. Information on 1564-hectare (3867-acre) Dyfi National Nature Reserve – its dunes, local history, wildlife, walks, etc.